Crochet
Adorned

• . • •. •

Crochet
Adorned

Reinvent Your Wardrobe with Crocheted Accents,
Embellishments, and Trims

Linda Permann

POTTER
CRAFT

NEW YORK

Published in the United States by Potter Craft,
an imprint of the Crown Publishing Group, a
division of Random House, Inc., New York.
www.crownpublishing.com
www.pottercraft.com

POTTER CRAFT and colophon is a registered
trademark of Random House, Inc.

Library of Congress Cataloging-in-Publication
Data

Permann, Linda.
    Crochet adorned : reinvent your wardrobe
with crocheted accents, embellishments,
and trims / Linda Permann.
        p.   cm.
    Includes index.
    ISBN 978-0-307-45196-5
    1. Crocheting.   2. Fancy work.   I. Title.
    TT820.P388   2009
    746.43'4—dc22   2008048077

Printed in China

Design by Kara Plikaitis
Photography by Heather Weston
Illustrations by woolypear

10 9 8 7 6 5 4 3 2 1

First Edition

Contributors

Tech Editing and Diagrams
Karen Manthey
Guest Designers
Tricia Royal (Mod Cross Pillow)
and *Diane Gilleland*
(Vintage Kitchen Trivets)
Stitch Pattern Swatches
Megan Granholm

*For Mom and Grandma—
thank you for continuing to
support my craftiness.*

Contents

Introduction

There is something so simple about sitting down with a hook, some yarn, and an idea. And yet the thought of making something to wear can be so intimidating! Notions of shaping stitches to fit your body, making sure you have the precise gauge, and wondering if you even measured yourself correctly in the first place can turn off beginners—and plenty of more experienced crafters!—from making crocheted garments.

Last summer I started thinking about ways to incorporate crochet into my wardrobe that took away the intimidation factor. I kept seeing crochet details in fashion and thinking, "I could do that . . . better." There's something about having a hand in making your garments that gives them longevity—for me, no store-bought piece can compete. So I started to design embellishment projects from simple trims to vintage-inspired, motif-based yokes and collars, and from there, this book was born. I hope you find the projects quick to work, inexpensive, and fun to make.

The wonderful thing about crocheting is that you only need to know how to make a few basic stitches in order to create a multitude of designs. Whether you're new to crocheting or a seasoned pro, get started with the first chapter of this book; it will teach you all about supplies, reading patterns and diagrams, and making basic stitches. If you've never worked with diagrams before, turn to Getting It Right (page 27) to learn how to read them. Stitch diagrams are a visual representation of every single crochet stitch, and if you learn visually, you'll likely find them much easier to follow than written instructions. The information in Custom Embellishing (page 32) and Finishing (page 35) wraps up how to apply the embellishment ideas in this book to your specific fashions.

The projects in this book are grouped according to use: Fashion, Accessories, and Home. The fashion projects all start with a "blank," a purchased garment you might already have or can easily acquire. Sometimes the blank is a basic tee, sometimes a sweater or skirt. The premise is this: if you start with something that fits, you won't have the typical worries that come with crocheting a garment. Let the finished project inspire your search, or start with a garment you want to refashion, then look through the book for the perfect embellishment. Remember that you don't always have to use the same blank I did—a trim shown on a jacket here could be just as pretty on your skirt. The accessory and home projects are made up of embellishment ideas (Like-New Shoes, anyone?), and things to make from scratch for that 100 percent do-it-yourself feeling. I've thrown in a little sewing for those of you who are multi-crafty, but don't worry, I also provide suggestions for starting with something readymade if you prefer.

Once you've worked your way through a few projects, I hope you'll be inspired to design your own. To that end, I've included a dictionary of different trims, motifs, and stitch patterns you can use to create your own looks. You might choose one stitch pattern to make the body of a scarf, and add a motif or two to decorate it. Or if you're a sewer, perhaps you'll just want to crochet a trim to accent your patchwork pillow—you can do that too! The dictionary is my exploration of stitch combinations, and I hope it inspires similar exploration in your projects. Feel free to mix and match your craft and crocheting skills with this wonderful stitch resource, and you will find that there really are no limits!

HERE'S TO CREATIVE CROCHETING!
—Linda

P.S.: I'd love to see your finished projects. Find me online at lindamade.com.

ONE
Techniques & Materials

Getting Started

One of the things I love most about crocheting is the very short supply list. All you really need to get started is a hook and some yarn. Many notions will come in handy as you develop your skills, but these two basic items are the most important tools.

ALL ABOUT HOOKS

Crochet hooks come in four varieties: aluminum, wood, plastic, and steel.

Though I admire delicate hand-carved wooden hooks, aluminum hooks are my favorite. They have nice smooth throats that yarn glides right over and, more importantly, they come in standard sizes (see chart, page 12). Until I started crocheting a *lot* I didn't realize that there are some noticeable differences among different kinds of aluminum hooks. Each brand has its own slightly different shape, and each is well suited for a particular kind of work, so go ahead and try a few different hooks when you're starting out—you may find one that feels more natural in your hand than another. For instance, hooks with a pointed tip make it easy to work into long foundation chains for projects like scarves and afghans. A rounded tip is helpful if you're working in the round and won't need to poke into your stitches as much, or when using a yarn that's liable to snag.

Wooden hooks are a luxurious option for crochet— you'll feel extra special when you work with them. The wood grips the yarn better than aluminum, which can be good if you're working with a slippery yarn, but annoying if you're working with fiber that tends to snag. Generally, wooden hooks are easier on your hands; they don't get as cold as metal, and the wood gives in to your grip ever so slightly, allowing you to hold the wooden hook more loosely. Wooden hooks are often handmade, so be sure to check their metric size if you're trying to match a gauge. Look for some fancy custom options if you want to treat yourself.

Plastic and its close relative, acrylic, are two other common materials used in affordable crochet hooks. These hooks are light and flexible like wooden hooks, only they are much less expensive. Personally, I fear that plastic hooks aren't always built to stand up to marathon crocheting, but they do come in every color of the rainbow (even glitter, if that's your thing), which is always fun. I tend to use them when I am crocheting super bulky yarn that requires a large hook—a hook made from any other material would be too heavy and unwieldy.

Last but not least are the tiny, strong steel hooks used for thread and lacework. You might have inherited a set of these silver beauties from a relative and wondered how she ever saw what she was doing. Although these tiny-diameter hooks can be intimidating, give them a shot to see the beautiful results they produce. Just to keep you guessing, steel hook labeling standards are the opposite of larger crochet hooks—the larger number on a steel hook indicates a smaller diameter, and it's not necessarily standard between brands, so check the metric measurement listed on the package. The difference in diameter between sizes is minuscule at times, so start out with two or three steel hooks and add other sizes to your collection if and when you need them.

Hook Sizes

U.S. Size	Metric Size
B-1	2.25 mm
C-2	2.75 mm
D-3	3.25 mm
E-4	3.5 mm
F-5	3.75 mm
G-6	4 mm
7	4.5 mm
H-8	5 mm
I-9	5.5 mm
J-10	6 mm
K-10½	6.5 mm
L-11	8 mm
M/N-13	9 mm
N/P-15	10 mm
P/Q	15 mm
Q	16 mm
S	19 mm

✳ Remember that steel hooks are sized differently—the larger the number, the smaller the hook. Steel hooks range in size from 14 to 00. Always choose a hook based on the metric measurement.

TIP: If you have a hook without a size label, put the shaft of the hook through a needle gauge (see supplies, page 14) to measure the diameter.

Hooks come in all shapes, sizes, and colors. Experiment with different types of hooks to see which one works best for you.

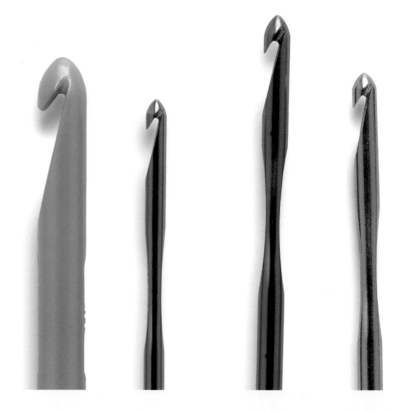

ANATOMY OF A HOOK ● ● ● ● ●

When you choose your first hooks, be sure to look at their form. Each brand and material has a slightly different shape to the tip and throat—some are rounded and some are cut in at a diagonal. It's up to you to decide which one you prefer, but you will probably discover that you do have a preference, and you might even change hook styles, depending on the project or type of yarn you are working with. If you're new to crocheting, try a few different brands of hooks as you go, rather than investing in a full set; that way you'll have a good idea of what works for you.

tip   shaft   handle

throat   grip

Hook Sizes

Crochet hooks come in standard sizes based on the metric measurement of their shaft diameter (see hook diagram, page 12). They're also labeled with letters that really don't mean much except that they give you a general idea of the size—B is the smallest diameter hook, S is the largest currently on the market. Steel hooks are labeled by number, but in the opposite direction—14 is the smallest diameter hook, 00 is the largest. To avoid unnecessary confusion, always choose your hook based on the metric measurement.

CHOOSING YARN

Everyone has an opinion on which fibers are the best, but here is my advice: Buy the best that you can afford, and buy what makes sense for the project.

There's no need to be a snob when it comes to fiber. Go with what looks good for your project—you might be surprised at some of the acrylic blends available today. With a little crochet flair, any basic yarn can shine. That said, a lot of the projects in this book are small and use less than a skein of yarn, so they're perfect for remnants you might already have or are a great excuse to splurge on a favorite fiber. For projects that use just a bit of six or seven colors, feel free to dive into your stash and use what you have on hand.

When you're buying yarn in person, do a couple of simple tests to see if the yarn will be a pleasure to work with. First, tug on a strand of your desired yarn to see if it has any stretch. Yarns with ease are, well, easy to work with—poking your hook through the stitches is simple and the resulting crocheted fabric will have a nice drape. Generally, a yarn with a touch of synthetic fibers mixed in will have a little stretch that's perfect for garments—remember how great it was when they started adding spandex to T-shirts?

The second thing you'll want to check is how well the yarn is plied—that is, how well does the strand stay together? Try pulling apart one strand of yarn, and if it splits without much effort, remember that it'll probably split just as easily while you are working with it. Skip the frustration and choose yarns that stay together.

The last test I like to do when buying yarn is the face test. It's probably best to do this in the corner of the store away from the register but, hey, you need to know how the yarn feels against your skin, so go ahead and touch it to your face to test the itch factor. The main reason that I don't buy yarn via the Internet is that there is no online face test. If you're making something to wear, it's important to know that it's not going to itch or otherwise irritate your skin. Sometimes it's hard to let go of a certain colorway or texture, but be realistic about wearability, because I'm sure you'll want to show off your new creation!

Substituting Yarns

The yarns used in this book serve as suggestions. There's a wide world of fiber options, so if you can't find a certain yarn or just plain don't like it, switch it! I can't completely guarantee your results if you deviate from the recommended yarn—some yards do weird things when they are blocked—but I'm pretty sure that your project will turn out fine and if not, you will learn something. For the best results when making substitutions, find something close to the suggested yarn by comparing both the weight and the yardage of the new yarn. It's also helpful to use the same fiber for results that are closest to the project shown. If you want to try a different fiber than the yarn listed in the project, please feel free to do so, but keep in mind that the new yarn should still be in the same weight category. Be aware that crocheted fabric may drape differently depending on the fiber used. Always make a gauge swatch to determine if the fiber is a good fit for the project (see page 30).

Yarn weight refers to the thickness of a strand of yarn. All yarns fall into the categories of the Yarn Substitution Chart (see page 14) but, annoyingly, not all yarns will tell you their weight category on the label. To be frank, you're going to have to do some guesswork when substituting yarns. To make it easier, compare the

Yarn Substitution Chart

Yarn Weight Symbol & Category Names	(0) LACE	(1) SUPER FINE	(2) FINE	(3) LIGHT	(4) MEDIUM	(5) BULKY	(6) SUPER BULKY
Type of Yarns in Category	Fingering 10-count crochet thread	Sock, Fingering, Baby	Sport, Baby	DK, Light Worsted	Worsted, Afghan, Aran	Chunky, Craft, Rug	Bulky, Roving
Crochet Gauge* Ranges in Single Crochet to 4 in.	32–42 double crochets**	21–32 sts	16–20 sts	12–17 sts	11–14 sts	8–11 sts	5–9 sts
Recommended Hook in Metric Size Range	Steel*** 1.6–1.4 mm	2.25–3.5 mm	3.5–4.5 mm	4.5–5.5 mm	5.5–6.5 mm	6.5–9 mm	9 mm and larger
Recommended Hook in U.S. Size Range	Steel*** 6, 7, 8 Regular hook B–1	B–1 to E–4	E–4 to 7	7 to I–9	I–9 to K–10 ½	K–10 ½ to M–13	M–13 and larger

* GUIDELINES ONLY: The above reflect the most commonly used gauges and needle or hook sizes for specific yarn categories.

** Lace-weight yarns are usually knitted or crocheted on larger needles and hooks to create lacy, openwork patterns. Accordingly, a gauge range is difficult to determine. Always follow the gauge stated in your pattern.

*** Steel crochet hooks are sized differently from regular hooks — the higher the number, the smaller the hook, which is the reverse of regular hook sizing.

(Source: Craft Yarn Council of America, www.YarnStandards.com)

suggested gauge on the label to the gauge for the project, or compare it to the gauge in the yarn weight category you're looking for. You might have to look at the knitting gauge, since not all companies are hip to crocheters yet. If it looks like a match, buy a ball and make a swatch before you get started—that way you'll have a clear idea of how the finished piece will look.

The yarn's yardage lets you know the total length of the yarn in the skein. Skeins don't come in standard lengths, so be sure to purchase enough yardage to match the amount recommended in the pattern. You may need more or fewer skeins than suggested, based on your substitute yarn's yardage. For instance, if the directions call for two 50-yard (46m) skeins, and your substitute skein contains 100 yards (91m), you'll only need one skein. Be sure to do the math, and if you're shopping locally, remember that most yarn shops will give you store credit for returned unused (and unwound) yarn, so it's a good idea to get the extra skein just in case.

SUPPLY STASH

Now that you've got your hooks and yarn in order, it's time to examine some of the other crochet and sewing tools that will make embellishing easier.

Yarn Needles

Available in both metal and plastic, these trusty tools are essential for weaving in your yarn ends. Select yarn needles with large eyes (for easy threading) and a blunt tip, which will prevent you from splitting yarn strands as you weave in the ends.

Needle Size Gauge

Although it was intended for knitters, this tool (pictured on page 15) is great for measuring hook size, too, especially if you have a lot of random hand-me-down hooks. Just slide the shaft of your hook through the holes until you find one that fits, and you'll know the diameter of your hook. A needle size gauge is also helpful for converting suggested knitting needle size to hook size—some yarn labels still don't list both measurements. You can also use the gauge for its other intended purpose: Lay the handy cut-out section over your work to accurately measure your gauge swatches.

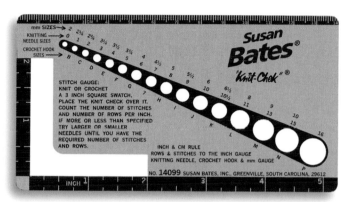

Stitch Markers

Stitch markers are invaluable for marking long foundation chains. Mark every 10, 20, or 30 stitches with a stitch marker as you go, and you won't have to count back from zero every time you pause. Use them to mark the right side of your work, the starting end of a trim, or a turning chain that counts as a stitch—that way you won't forget it! I also use stitch markers to secure the last loop of my work when I stop in the middle of a project. Be sure to buy stitch markers with a split ring or clasp construction so you can easily remove them when you need to. If you don't want to spend any money, just use a small length of contrasting yarn to mark your stitches instead. And if you've never used a stitch marker before, try it—they really will help you keep your project on track.

Measuring Tape

You'll need a handy measuring tape to help determine the length of the necklines, hems, and waistbands you'll be embellishing. Be sure to use a flexible tape, as opposed to a ruler, when measuring curved areas.

Scissors

A good pair of small, sharp scissors will make it easy to trim your yarn ends. Stash them where you work so you can find them easily.

You'll also need to invest in fabric scissors or a rotary cutter and mat if you're going to try your hand at some of the sewing projects, such as the Floral Motif Yoke Top (page 61) or the Butterfly apron (page 96). Hide both pairs of scissors from anyone who might use them to cut something other than fiber; that way they'll stay sharp.

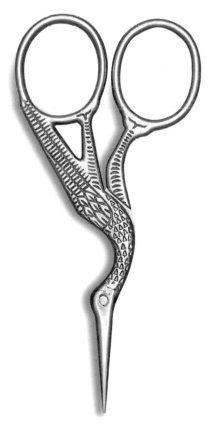

Iron

A reliable iron is essential for blocking and for pressing sewn seams. Choose an iron with a variable steam setting and a variety of temperatures.

T-Pins

These sturdy, rustproof pins are essential to help you ease your crocheted garment into shape when blocking. They're shaped like a T to hold your work in place, and they won't melt under the heat of an iron. Skip the craft store and buy these in bulk at the office supply store instead—they're much cheaper there.

Straight Pins and Sewing Needles

Use straight pins to attach trims and motifs to your garments. They will help you determine your design layout and hold your embellishments in place while you sew them on. Choose sharp needles that will easily pierce your fabric. Stash them both in a cute pincushion to keep them in order—and out of the couch cushions!

Seam Ripper

This inexpensive sewing tool will come in handy when you're deconstructing garments. The sharp tip makes it easy to rip and remove threads in a snap.

Sewing Thread

Good-quality thread makes it simple to attach trims and motifs to your garments. To get the closest match, bring a sample of your yarn or garment (depending which you're matching) to the store when buying thread. Cotton and polyester blends are great for sewing crochet accents in place—the polyester gives the thread a bit of added strength.

Sewing Machine

Although a sewing machine is not essential for attaching embellishments, it's handy for the projects that involve construction sewing.

Crochet Basics: Stitches, Seams, and Blocking

Amazingly, the majority of crocheted items are made from different combinations of four basic stitches: single, half double, double, and treble. Learn the proper hook- and yarn-holding techniques first, then proceed to stitch making. If you get frustrated, don't give up! Make a visit to your local yarn shop to ask for hands-on help, or search the Internet for stitch videos. Practice makes perfect.

HOLDING THE HOOK

There are a couple of different ways to hold the crochet hook. If you already have a method that works for you, continue to use it. If not, try both of the following methods and see which one feels more comfortable to you.

Method 1: Hold the hook in your hand like a knife, as shown below, using your thumb and forefinger to maneuver the hook.

Method 2: Hold the hook in your hand like a pen, as shown below, working downward into the stitches.

HOLDING THE YARN

All of us develop our own way to hold the yarn. When I started out, I would try to pinch it between my left thumb and forefinger, which led to lots of hand cramps with little success. Then I learned this yarn-holding technique, which makes it easy to feed the yarn at a steady tension. It's not for everyone, so if you already practice a technique that's comfortable for you, by all means, run with it. If you're a beginner, though, I suggest you give this a try.

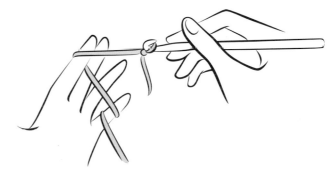

With your left palm facing you, wrap the tail end of the yarn around your pinky finger from front to back to front. Next, bring the yarn up to the space between your middle and index finger. Slip the yarn behind your index finger and bring it back to the front of your palm. When you're just starting a chain, hold the yarn this way and pinch the slipknot on the hook between your left thumb and index finger. Use your index finger to create tension by tugging the yarn tight or loosening your grip. When you need more yarn, just wiggle your fingers!

MAKING A SLIPKNOT

You'll start each foundation chain with a basic slipknot.

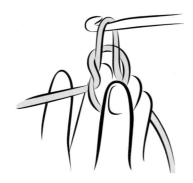

To make a slipknot: Leaving an 8" (20.5cm) tail, make a loop with your yarn. Use your hook or your finger to catch the ball end of the yarn and draw this yarn through the loop. Tighten the yarn around the shaft of your crochet hook by tugging on the yarn tail.

MAKING THE FOUNDATION CHAIN

The foundation chain is the first row of chain stitches you'll make when you start a project worked in rows. Follow the directions (right) to learn how to make the chain stitch, and how to properly count the number of stitches in the foundation chain. You will also use chain stitches throughout some crochet designs. Make these chain stitches in the same way. Often they will be referred to in subsequent rounds by the number of chains followed by loop or space, for instance, a "ch-5 lp" (chain 5 loop) or "ch-5 sp" (chain 5 space).

> TIP: When making a long foundation chain, mark every 10th stitch with a stitch marker. This will make it easy to see how many stitches you have made at a glance, without having to count from zero every time you pause.

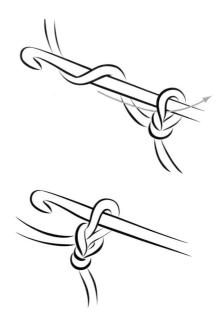

To start the foundation chain, make a slipknot and place it on your hook. Hold the hook in your right hand and the yarn in your left. Wrap the yarn over the hook from the back to the front of the hook; this is called a yarn over. Catch the yarn in the hook's throat and draw the hook and yarn loop through the loop on your hook.

Slide the new loop to the shaft of your hook to complete one chain stitch. Repeat this process, making a yarn over and drawing it through the loop on your hook, for as many chains as indicated.

To count chain stitches, hold the chain vertically so that the V shapes of the stitches are lined up. Do not count the original slipknot or the loop still on the hook; everything else is a stitch. There are 5 stitches on the chain above.

WORKING THE FOUNDATION CHAIN ● ● ● ● ●

There are several ways to insert your hook into the foundation chain to make your first row of stitches. Traditionally, the hook is inserted under the "V" of each chain stitch, as detailed in the instructions for all of the stitch heights in this chapter, but sometimes that method can be tricky. Here are two alternate ways to work the foundation chain. Both are fine to use, just be consistent and use the same technique to work the entire first row of stitches.

Working into the "V" of the Foundation Chain

Here's a method that's easy for beginners. Turn the chain so that the Vs are facing you. Insert your hook into the V, catching the top of the V and the bottom loop of the chain (the small loop under the V), as shown, then make your stitch as directed.

Working the Bottom of the Foundation Chain

Another technique involves working into the bottom of the chain. Turn your chain so that the underside loops are facing you and insert your hook under the loop (above the V) of the first stitch. Make your stitch as directed.

I like to work my first rows this way when I make trims, because it produces a pretty double-looped bottom edge. Essentially you'll have Vs on both sides of the foundation chain after you complete your first row. You can also use this method when you're crocheting pieces that you know you will join or add a border to later. Of course, the reason I really like to work my chains this way is that it's much easier to slide the hook under the bottom of the chain than into the strands of the V.

Remember, you should only use these alternate methods on the first row of stitches. For stitches that aren't worked in the foundation chain, always work under the V of the stitch. It's a cinch once you're past the foundation row.

SINGLE CROCHET (SC)

The single crochet is the shortest stitch, and is sometimes referred to as the "plain" stitch.

To make a single crochet, insert your hook from front to back under both strands of the V shape of the second chain from your hook. Wrap the yarn over the hook and draw it through the foundation chain, leaving two loops on the hook.

Yarn over once more and draw the yarn through both loops on the hook to complete one single crochet. Work one single crochet in each stitch of the row. When you complete the row, turn the work, make one chain for the turning chain (this does *not* count as a stitch), and continue to work the next row of single crochet stitches. Inserting your hook under the two loops of the V at the top of each stitch, work one single crochet in each stitch across, and remember to skip the turning chain.

HALF DOUBLE CROCHET (HDC)

The next tallest stitch is the half double crochet. You'll wrap the yarn around the hook before you insert it into the stitch to make a taller stitch.

To make a half double crochet, yarn over and insert the hook from front to back under the V of the third chain from your hook. Yarn over again and draw the yarn through the foundation chain.

You should have three loops on the hook. Yarn over and draw the yarn through all three loops to complete one half double crochet. You now have one half double crochet and a turning chain (the two chains you skipped at the beginning of the foundation chain make up the turning chain, and they count as one stitch). Work one half double crochet in each chain across, then turn the work. Chain 2 for the turning chain, which counts as the first half double crochet of the next row. Skip the first half double crochet at the beginning of the row and half double crochet in each stitch across the row, including the second chain of the turning chain.

DOUBLE CROCHET (DC)

The double crochet stitch is my personal favorite—it's tall and fast, perfect for quick projects.

To make a double crochet, yarn over and insert the hook from front to back under the V of the fourth stitch from your hook. Yarn over again and draw the yarn through the foundation chain loop.

You now have three loops on your hook. Yarn over and draw the yarn through the first two loops.

Two loops remain on your hook. Yarn over once more and draw the yarn through the last two loops. You've made one double crochet and one turning chain (the three chains you skipped at the beginning of the foundation chain are the turning chain, and they count as one stitch). Complete the row of double crochet stitches, turn the work, and chain 3 to count as your turning chain. Skip the first double crochet of the row and double crochet in each stitch across, including one stitch in the third chain of the turning chain.

TREBLE CROCHET (TR)

The treble crochet is even taller than the double crochet—you'll wrap the yarn around the hook twice to achieve this new height.

To make a treble crochet, yarn over the hook twice and insert the hook under the V shape of the fifth chain stitch from your hook. Yarn over again and draw the loop through foundation chain loop.

You now have four loops on your hook. Yarn over and draw a loop through the first two loops, leaving three loops on the hook. Yarn over again and draw through the next two loops—now two loops remain. Yarn over once more and draw through the final two loops. You've made one treble crochet and one turning chain (the four chains you skipped at the beginning of the foundation chain make up the turning chain, and they count as one stitch). Work one treble crochet in each chain across. When you reach the end of the row, turn the work, and chain 4 to count as your turning chain. Skip the first treble crochet and treble in each stitch across, including one stitch in the fourth chain of the turning chain.

WHAT ARE TURNING CHAINS AND BEGINNING CHAINS? • • • • •

A turning chain is the number of chains you work at the beginning of each row to account for the height of different crochet stitches. When working in rows, you can make the chain before or after you turn the work to start a new row; it's really up to you, just remember to be consistent. When you are working in the round, this chain is called the *beginning chain*. It holds the same purpose—to get your work up to the proper height for the stitch you are using—but since you don't typically turn work done in the round, it has a slightly different name.

Make the following number of turning or beginning chains for each stitch:

Single Crochet	Chain 1
Half Double Crochet	Chain 2
Double Crochet	Chain 3
Treble Crochet	Chain 4

In this book, the turning and beginning chains are counted as the first stitch of the row or round except in the case of single crochet stitches. That means that when you come across a turning chain from the previous row or round, you should count it as a stitch and therefore stitch into the last chain of the turning chain as you come across it. If the first piece you work in rows looks like a triangle instead of a square, it's likely that you forgot to stitch into your turning chains as you worked.

SLIP STITCH

A slip stitch doesn't add any noticeable height to your work and is used to join rounds of crochet. Slip stitches can also be used to move the hook position and to neaten the edges of finished crochet pieces.

To make a slip stitch, insert the hook under the V in the second stitch from your hook. Yarn over and draw this loop through the V, then through the loop on your hook to complete the slip stitch. Continue to work this way through as many stitches as indicated by the pattern.

WORKING IN THE ROUND

Many crochet motifs are worked outward from the center, or "in the round." I love to crochet in the round because it doesn't require long foundation chains, and it's so much easier to get your hook through a stitch than through a foundation chain.

Work in the round always starts with a ring. The first way to make a ring is to make a short foundation chain and join the first and last chain with a slip stitch. This makes a sturdy ring, perfect for motifs with open centers. When working into a chain ring, work the stitches over the whole chain (rather than into specific stitches) unless the pattern indicates otherwise.

The second way to start is to make a "magic ring." A magic ring lets you crochet over an adjustable loop (unlike the fixed size of a chain loop) and then pull the loop tight at the end so that there is no hole in the center of your work.

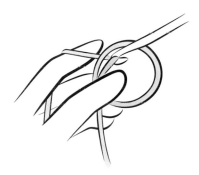

and continue crocheting. Remember to leave long tails of both the old and new yarn so you can weave them in securely.

To change colors seamlessly, join the new color of yarn in the last yarn over of the stitch *before* the stitch you want worked in the new color. For example, if you're working a row of pink double crochet stitches and want to change to purple yarn starting with the next stitch, stop working when you have the final two loops of your last pink double crochet on the hook. Yarn over with the purple yarn and complete the last pink double crochet. Continue stitching with your new purple yarn.

To make a magic ring, leaving an 8" (20.5cm) tail, make a loop with the yarn by placing the tail end behind the ball end of the yarn. Grasp the place where the yarn overlaps between your thumb and forefinger. Insert your hook through the loop and draw up a loop (being sure to use the ball end of the yarn). Without tightening the original loop, chain the directed number of stitches and then work the remaining stitches of the round into the loop. Join the first round, then pull on the tail end of the yarn to tighten the center.

FASTENING OFF

When you've finished the last crochet stitch and are ready to secure it, cut the yarn from the ball, leaving an 8–12" (20.5–30.5cm) tail. I like to err on the side of a long tail, since some yarn can be pesky to weave in, and there's no way to lengthen a too-short yarn tail. The longer length also comes in handy for sewing motifs together.

After working each round of stitches (whether you're using a magic ring or a chain ring), join the first stitch to the last with a slip stitch. Continue working on the next round—you don't need to turn the piece when working in the round.

JOINING YARNS

When you want to change colors or move to a new ball of yarn, you will need to join the new yarn to your work. Joining yarn is simple: Make the last stitch with the old yarn until you reach the last yarn over of the stitch. Make the last yarn over with the new yarn, complete the stitch,

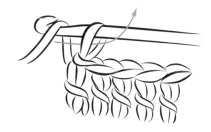

To fasten off, yarn over and draw the yarn tail through the last loop on your hook. Tug on the yarn to tighten the loop.

WEAVING IN ENDS

Once you've fastened off the yarn tail, it's time to weave in the yarn ends. Thread the yarn tail through a blunt

DIFFERENTIATING BETWEEN RIGHT AND WRONG SIDE • • • • •

For crochet worked in rows, including trims and stitch patterns, the side of the work facing you as you work the first row is considered the "Right Side" of the work unless the pattern tells you otherwise. You may want to mark the first row with a stitch marker as you are working it so that it will be easy to distinguish between the sides later. Because you turn work crocheted in rows, when the first row is the Right Side row, the second row is the Wrong Side, third is Right Side, and so on. Certain stitch combinations may indicate different right and wrong sides of the work, and in these cases you will notice Wrong Side (WS) and Right Side (RS) abbreviations at the beginning of each pattern row.

For patterns worked in the round, unless otherwise indicated, the "Right Side" of the work is the side facing you throughout the work. Since most crochet worked in the round is never turned, the Right Side of each round of stitches will face you. In certain cases, for instance, when making bobble stitches (which puff toward the back of the work), the pattern will indicate to turn the work to the Wrong Side, work the round, and then turn it back to the Right Side for the next round. Pay attention to the RS and WS abbreviations at the beginning of these rounds to correctly stitch the pattern.

Always take the time to locate the right side of the work before attaching it to your piece—ripping seams is no fun.

Once you see the difference blocking makes, you'll never skip it again.
Above, compare an unblocked motif (left) to a blocked motif (right).

yarn needle and weave the end through five or six stitches on the wrong side of the work. Reverse the direction of the needle, skip one stitch, and weave back through those same stitches you just went through for a secure end. When you have multiple ends in the same area, try to weave them through different stitches so no one section gets too bulky.

BLOCKING TRIMS AND MOTIFS

The next, essential step to a fabulous crochet piece is blocking. Usually just the mention of blocking inspires groans in crocheters and knitters alike, but it really makes a difference in the look of your finished piece. If you've never blocked your work before, try it. I'm certain that once you see the difference you'll never skip it again.

Blocking literally gets your stitches into shape by relaxing the fibers so that they lay as you've arranged them. You can use blocking to standardize motif size, which is especially helpful if you're sewing them together. Most of the projects in this book are relatively small and you can block them on your ironing board.

Before you get started, check your yarn label for specific blocking instructions, such as which heat setting to use on your iron. If there's no information and you're working with a natural fiber, use the iron's recommended setting, based on the fiber content of the yarn, and a high steam setting. If the fiber is synthetic, do *not* block it with your iron. Instead, use the spray blocking method outlined below.

> TIP: Always remember: Blocking is *not* ironing. Fibers will flatten when pressed with a warm iron, so *never* let the iron touch your yarn.

Blocking Tools

In order to block you'll need these four things:

Blocking Surface You can purchase a blocking board complete with a grid and measurements if you want to get technical, but any padded surface will do. I like to block on my ironing board. I protect it with a second cover I use only for blocking—keep in mind that over time the cover will be riddled with pin holes. If you don't have an ironing board, you may also use a blanket or towel folded over several times to create a padded surface. I've also seen people block right on their mattress or carpet—just be sure to lay a press cloth between the work surface and your work to avoid any stains.

Spray Bottle Fill a spray bottle with water and use it to lightly spray your crocheted work before easing it into shape. You will also use the spray bottle for spray blocking.

T-Pins These are rustproof pins that won't melt under the heat of the iron, and they're shaped like a T to hold your work in place. You may need quite a few T-pins to get a lacy design just right.

Steam Iron For the best results, use an iron that produces a lot of steam. Remember that you won't ever let the iron touch the piece; instead you will hold the iron at least two inches (5cm) above the work and infuse it with steam.

Blocking Natural Fibers

To block your work, first spray it lightly with the water from the spray bottle. Next, gently ease and pin it into shape with T-pins. If you are blocking several motifs, set them up next to one another to make sure they are all the same size. I usually eyeball the size, but you can use a ruler to check the measurements if you like.

Once all of the crocheted pieces are pinned in place, hold your steam iron (set to the appropriate heat setting based on fiber content) two to three inches (5–7.5cm) above the surface of your work. Hover over the work in sections, steaming each section for about ten seconds. Turn off the iron and let the piece dry completely, sometimes overnight, before you remove the pins.

Spray Blocking Acrylic Fibers

When you work with acrylic or synthetic fibers, use a spray bottle to moisten the pinned-out piece. Do not block acrylic fibers with steam, as the heat may cause some yarns to melt. Allow the moistened piece to dry before you remove the pins.

JOINING MOTIFS

After you make and block your motifs, chances are you'll
need to attach them to each other; this is called *joining* or
seaming. There are several ways to join pieces together,
but these two are my favorite.

Slip Stitch Join

This join works best for pieces with long, straight edges.
It's also easy to pull out if you make a mistake.

Place two motifs together with their right sides facing;
line up the stitches on the edge you will join. To make
an even join, count the number of stitches on the edge

of each motif and make sure they match. Starting at the
right side of the edge, insert your hook under the V of
one stitch on both pieces, yarn over, and pull up the yarn
through the stitches and the loop on the hook to make a
slip stitch. Continue to work a slip stitch through the back
loops of the edge stitches for the entire edge (or length of
the join). Leave your yarn tail long if you're joining this
piece to another, or weave in the ends.

Whipstitch

The whipstitch is a sturdy join I use for round and oddly
shaped motifs. Often, I'll sew a few stitches of two motifs
together, weave the joining yarn through one of the
motifs to move it to the next area that needs to be joined,
and then sew another section together.

To make a whipstitch join, place two motifs together

with their right sides facing and line up the stitches you
wish to join. If you're working with a square motif, be
sure to line up the corners of the square.

Thread a blunt yarn needle with yarn to match the
motifs you are joining and begin stitching at the right-
hand side of the work. Leaving a long yarn tail, insert the
needle through one stitch of each of the two motifs you
are joining and pull the yarn taut to complete one whipstitch. Insert the needle through the next stitch of both
motifs, and pull taut. Continue stitching in this manner.
You may also make the whipstitch through only the outer
loops of the stitches you are joining, to form a nice,
structured seam. When you are finished whipstitching
the areas you'd like to join, weave in the yarn ends.

Getting It Right

Now that you're familiar with basic stitches, let me introduce you to the parts and abbreviations contained in patterns. Crochet patterns can be frustrating at first—all of the abbreviations can make the written instructions sound like a stutter. But once you learn how to read them, they're really pretty simple—they tell you exactly what to do.

ANATOMY OF A CROCHET PATTERN

Skill Level

The skill level indicates the amount of crocheting and, if relevant, sewing experience you'll need to complete a project. Take this as a suggestion, but don't let it stop you from trying something new. After all, the only way you will learn new skills is to advance to projects with higher skill levels.

Finished Size

This section lays out the final dimensions of a project. Since the projects in this book are made to order, the finished size can usually be tweaked to your specific purpose. Details on how to change the size are included here and in the pattern.

Materials

Here you'll find a list of what you will need to make the project, and specific information about hook size and yarn weight. Use the CYCA yarn weight listed in this section to make any yarn substitutions you'd like.

Gauge

Here's a breath of fresh air: Gauge is *not critical* for most projects in this book. As in, the project isn't likely to *not fit* if you don't follow it exactly. However, it is good idea to get in the habit of checking your gauge. This section will tell you how to crochet a gauge swatch and what the finished swatch should measure. A gauge swatch will give you a good idea of the size of each motif or section, and it will show you how the crocheted fabric drapes. Match the gauge with your hook and yarn for the best results, especially if you are making a yarn substitution.

Special Stitches

This section will define any special stitches or combinations that aren't included on the standard abbreviation list or in the section beginning on page 20.

Pattern

The pattern contains all the directions you'll need to construct your project. It's a good idea to read through *the whole pattern* before you get started—that way you'll know where you're headed. It can be helpful to make a photocopy of the pattern you're using so that you can mark it up to help keep track of where you are or note any changes you make. Highlight rows as you go so you won't get lost, or move a sticky note line by line as you progress. If you stop in the middle of a pattern, make a note of where you left off so it's easy to start again.

Stitch Diagrams

I've included stitch diagrams throughout the book to make instructions exceptionally clear. Turn to page 29 for more information about how to read and understand stitch diagrams.

Abbreviations

To really understand a pattern, you'll need to familiarize yourself with the abbreviations. The patterns in this book use standard crochet abbreviations as listed in the chart. Refer to this list if you're unsure what each abbreviation stands for. For those of you in England or Australia, I've also included a conversion chart, since we call our stitches by different names.

Standard Crochet Abbreviations	
BL	work stitches in the back loops only
ch	chain
dc	double crochet
FL	work stitches in the front loops only
hdc	half double crochet
lp(s)	loop(s)
RS	right side of work
sc	single crochet
sk	skip
sl st	slip stitch
sp(s)	space(s)
tog	together
tr	treble crochet
WS	wrong side of work
yo	yarn over (wrap yarn over hook)
* ;	Repeat directions between * and ; as many times as indicated.
( )	Work directions inside parentheses into the stitch indicated.
[ ]	Work the directions inside the brackets as many times as indicated.

Conversion Chart	
U.S. TERM	**U.K./AUS TERM**
dc double crochet	**tr** treble crochet
hdc half double crochet	**htr** half treble crochet
sc single crochet	**dc** double crochet
sl st slip stitch	**sc** single crochet
tr treble crochet	**dtr** double treble crochet

UNDERSTANDING WRITTEN PATTERNS

Patterns can be intimidating, so once you read through them for the general idea, remember to take them one line at a time. Be sure to refer to the abbreviation chart in order to understand the patterns in this book, and refer to the stitch diagrams for a visual representation of what you're doing.

In addition to knowing the stitch abbreviations, you'll also need to learn the shorthand used in the patterns in this book.

First, notice that there is a summation of stitches at the end of each row or round. For instance, your pattern might say:

> **Round 1** Ch 3 (counts as dc), 9 dc in ring, sl st in top of beginning ch to join—10 dc.

The "10 dc" at the end of the round tells you how many stitches were made in this round so that you can double check your work by counting stitches. It does *not* mean that you should ch 3 (counts as dc), make 9 dc, and then make another 10 dc in the ring. It means that you chained 3, which counted as 1 dc, then worked 9 double crochets into the ring, for a grand total of 10 dc.

When you are forming patterns with different stitch heights, usually the summation is simplified and might not include every stitch in the round. The summation gives you a general idea so you can check your work at a glance, for example:

Round 4 *(Ch 1, hdc, dc, hdc, ch 1, sl st, ch 1, hdc, dc, hdc, ch 1) in next ch-4 lp, sl st in next sc; repeat from * around, sl st in first sl st to join—12 petals.

The instructions in parentheses form each "petal," and you should have repeated them 12 times around. This might seem fuzzy while you are reading it, but when you begin working rounds it will become clearer.

Another abbreviation you'll come across in most patterns is a group of stitches in parentheses, like this:

(hdc, dc, ch 1) in next stitch.

In this case, the parentheses tell you to work the half double crochet, the double crochet, and the chain 1 all in the same stitch. Sometimes the parentheses will contain multiple stitches worked over a loop; the parentheses make it easy to group the stitches together so you won't get lost.

Parentheses (or brackets) can also indicate that you're going to repeat the instruction in parentheses a certain number of times. For instance:

(tr, ch 1) twice in next dc.

This means that you will (treble, chain 1, treble, chain 1) in the next dc of the round.

Another common abbreviation you'll run into is the asterisk. The asterisk is also used to mark a set of instructions that will be repeated. In most patterns in this book, the instructions to be repeated are marked off with an asterisk (*) at the beginning and followed by a semicolon (;) at the end, like this:

Ch 3, dc in first stitch, ch 2, *2 dc in next dc, ch 2; repeat from * around, sl st in top of beginning ch to join—10 ch-2 spaces.

For this round, chain 3, double crochet in the first stitch, chain 2, then work 2 dc in the next dc, chain 2, make 2 dc in the following dc, ch 2, and so on, until you reach the end of the round. This is another example of why it's helpful to have the summation at the end of the round or row—if you are ever confused about what to

repeat, you can compare the directions and the summation to make sure they match.

In a few patterns, you will see an asterisk (*) marking the beginning and end of one set of instructions and a set of 2 asterisks (**) marking the beginning and end of another set of instructions, all in the same round. See below:

*ch 3, sk next stitch, sc in next stitch *; repeat from * to * 17 times, **ch 1, sk next stitch, sc in next stitch **; repeat from ** to ** 12 times.

The double asterisk is used to distinguish one set of repeated stitches from another, because sometimes you will repeat both sets of instructions in the round. Here you will (chain 3, skip the next stitch, single crochet in the next stitch) 17 times, then begin 12 repeats of the instructions flanked by double asterisks.

That's really all there is to it! Now that you know all about the anatomy, abbreviations, and shorthand secrets contained in patterns, you should be crocheting in no time. Use the written directions in combination with the stitch diagrams to make crocheting extra simple.

DECODING STITCH DIAGRAMS

A stitch diagram is a visual representation of the crochet stitches in a project. Stitch diagrams are included with every pattern in this book, because, to me, they are *so* much easier to understand than written instructions. The diagrams provide the exact same instructions as written instructions, and in most cases you can use the diagrams exclusively if you prefer. Just keep in mind that it is sometimes necessary to refer to the written instructions for information on assembling motifs or adding solid areas of simple crochet stitches. If you are confused by written directions, compare the written instructions with the diagram for clarification. To use the diagrams, study the symbols on page 31 so that you become familiar with them. Stitch keys are also provided with each diagram, so you won't have to keep flipping back here.

Each symbol in the diagram stands for a single stitch

or instruction, and its placement within the diagram indicates exactly where to work it. Some symbols stand for a cluster or group of stitches, such as a bobble. These symbols are linked to show they are joined, and a definition explaining how to make the special stitch is included in the written pattern instructions.

Understanding Diagrams Worked in the Round

The diagrams for motifs worked in the round start in the center with either the symbol for a magic ring or a ring of chains. The diagram continues outward with each round, which is just the way you'll crochet.

Each round is numbered to the *right* of the first stitch or beginning chain. Follow the diagram around *counterclockwise* to make the stitches in the correct order for each round. In certain cases, the round is numbered to the *left* of the first stitch and labeled with an arrow pointing to the right. This indicates that the round is worked on the wrong side of your motif, so you'll need to turn your work before beginning the round. You will still make the stitches in this round *counterclockwise* around the crochet work, but you will follow the wrong side rounds of the diagram *clockwise* to work the stitches correctly. The reason the wrong side rounds are shown clockwise in the diagram (even though, again, you are crocheting around counterclockwise) is that the diagram represents the way the work will look when viewed from the right side. Remember to turn the work (if indicated) back to the right side when you're finished with the wrong side round(s).

In this book, alternate rounds are shown in different colors to make the diagrams easy to read.

Understanding Diagrams for Patterns Worked in Rows

Stitch patterns—that is, groups of stitches that form a design over the crocheted fabric—are worked and shown row by row, as are the trims in this book. Read the patterns as if you're looking at the front of the fabric. Each pattern starts with the foundation chain (read left to right). The right-side rows (Rows 1, 3, 5, etc.) are read from right to left—just the way you'll be working your stitches. Wrong-side rows (2, 4, 6, etc.) are read from left to right since they are worked on the wrong side of the work and the diagram shows what the front side of the fabric will look like. Row numbers are listed on the starting side of each row to prevent any confusion, so for rows numbered on the right, read right to left, and for rows numbered on the left, read left to right. In this book, alternating rows are shown in different colors for clarity.

MAKING GAUGE

I saved the best, most important thing, for last: the dreaded gauge swatch! Here's the good news: For most of the projects in this book, you won't feel like you are working a bunch of gauge swatches for nothing. Usually you can work up the first motif or a few repeats of a trim pattern and measure it against the gauge. If it doesn't match up, you can always save the motif for a decoration on another project. If it does match, you're one step closer to finishing the project. Don't stress yourself out if your gauge is just slightly off. If you like the way your motif looks and feels, and you think it will work well repeated in the way the pattern suggests, try it!

To make a swatch, work the indicated stitch or pattern portion with the suggested hook size. If the swatch is too big, try a smaller hook size. If the swatch is too small, try a larger hook. You're aiming for a swatch that matches the listed measurements. It may take a few tries to get it right, but making a gauge swatch will give you a clear idea of what you'll end up with, and that will make the swatching time totally worth it—trust me!

Even if you don't work a swatch to match my gauge (for instance, if you're trying it with a much thinner or thicker yarn), you should work one to get a feel for the fabric you're producing and to make sure that that the trim or embellishment will work well with your garment. For instance, if you were making the trim from the Scalloped Spring Jacket with a superfine yarn, it'd be helpful to know approximately how many scallops there

STITCH KEY

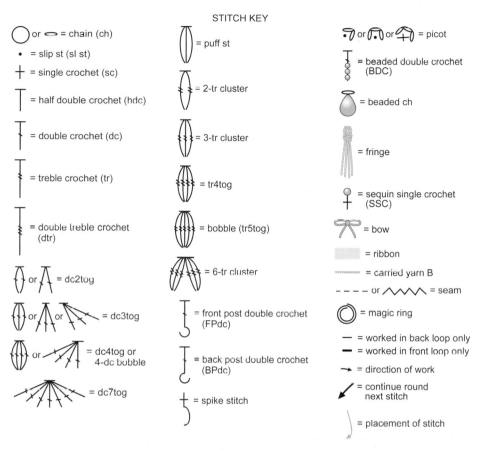

This chart lists all of the stitches used in the diagrams throughout this book. It's perfectly fine to work with diagrams only—just remember that you can also refer to the written instructions if you get confused.

were per inch (2.5cm) of trim. Not only will working a gauge swatch help you to determine that, but by working one you'll end up producing a small sample you can hold against your garment to make sure it looks good. If you're working with yarn you have on hand, you can even make a swatch first, then take the swatch to the store to find the perfect garment to match it. Look at it this way: A gauge swatch is actually a much better use of time than, say, crocheting a 40" (101.5cm) long trim and realizing it doesn't suit you.

The concept of gauge is actually quite practical. You make a swatch to match the designed garment using a hook size *that works for you.* I know it's tempting to just get started already, but when you work a gauge swatch first you can stitch confidently with the right hook and yarn for the project instead of having to constantly be aware of how loose or tight your stitches are. Making gauge means you can stitch it your way with your hook and your yarn and still end up with the same results. What could be better?

Custom Embellishing

Picking the garment you'll decorate is just as important as choosing your yarn. Most projects will list what type of garment to look for, but consider the tips in this section before you go shopping. I'll also explain how to translate your garment's measurements into an embellishment that's a perfect fit.

CHOOSING YOUR CANVAS: WHAT TO EMBELLISH

First and foremost, in case this wasn't obvious: Pick a garment that fits you well. The whole idea is to embellish something that already fits so you won't have to wonder if the final project will flatter you. It's okay to spend a little bit of money, even on something you're going to change, because you won't enjoy wearing your finished piece unless it was comfortable and stylish in the first place. The projects in this book are perfect for refashioning thrift-store finds and things lurking in the back of your closet. You know the ones: They still fit, but you're bored with them, and yet you can't bring yourself to give them away. Embellishments can do wonders to give a garment new life. In addition to making something feel "fresh," they can hide small stains or rips in the garment (think *Pretty in Pink*).

The second thing to remember is that blank doesn't have to mean boring. A basic tee or tank will work fine for many of these projects, but something with stripes or a little printed texture might prove to add complexity and even more style to your finished design. Think outside the box and browse fashion magazines for examples of layered textures.

Another thing to consider is ease. When it comes to skirts and dresses, avoid elastic waistlines—and I'm not just saying that from a style standpoint! Crocheted trims are not going to stretch the way an elastic waistband does, so applying the static trim to the stretchy skirt may lead to disaster. Garments that have zippers are easier to

embellish because you can butt the trim right up to the zipper and avoid the stretch issue altogether. Another tip: Look for garments that are easy to move in—if it's already tight or difficult to put on, it's possible you could snap the threads that attach your embellishments as you get dressed. Avoid this disappointment by choosing wisely from the beginning.

Finally, consider which cut works best for the embellishments you want to add. There are endless options for embellishing: skirt waists or hems, pockets, plackets, sleeves, collars, and more. Different cuts will make certain garments easier to transform. For example, if you wanted to place a few rows of inset trim on a skirt, a tiered skirt would be the best way to start. It already has seams where each tier begins, so it should be easy enough to deconstruct. Starting with a too large straight skirt, on the other hand, might leave you with too little fabric and oddly placed tiers. Whenever possible, work with the details on your garment to determine how you're going to arrange your embellishments.

WHICH CAME FIRST: THE GARMENT OR THE YARN?

After making all of the projects in this book, I can tell you that it's easiest to find the garment first, then find a yarn that coordinates. There are more colors, brands, and textures of yarn available than there are basic garments. Plus, the shape of your shirt will give you an idea about how you want to embellish it—which is a good thing to know before you shop for yarn. If you're shopping this way, *take the garment with you* when you buy yarn. As much as you try, you will never remember the color exactly in your head, and it's frustrating to have a near match. If the yarn shop is dimly lit, don't be afraid to ask to take a skein of yarn outside so you can see if it really matches your garment.

On the other hand, these projects do lend themselves to using up single skeins from your stash, so if you already have the yarn you need, tuck a length of it into your purse when you shop. You may even want to work up a test swatch—that is, a couple of motifs or a short length of trim—to take with you. Hold the swatch up to the garment you're considering to get a true idea of the finished look.

BEFORE YOU START: IT'S A WASH ● • ● ● ● ●

Before you get started, be sure to wash any new garments or fabric just in case they shrink. If you're embellishing an item that will only be dry cleaned or hand-washed, such as a jacket or purse, it's okay to skip this step.

DETERMINING FOUNDATION CHAIN LENGTH

The trim patterns in this book are written so that you can work a trim of any length. Some trims are worked side to side in short rows that add length as you work them— these are the easy ones. Other trims require you to work a long foundation row before you get started on the pattern. For these trims, it's important to figure out just how long to make your foundation chain so that you'll end up with the right length of trim.

To determine how many chains you'll need to work in the foundation chain, make a gauge swatch. Measure the length of the gauge swatch and the length of one pattern repeat (for instance, a shell, bobble, or other stitch combination). Divide the swatch length by the number of repeats in your gauge swatch. For instance, if there are 6 shells in your 3" (7.5cm) swatch,

3" (7.5cm) / 6 shells = ½" (13mm) per shell repeat

Next, divide the length of trim you need (for instance, 20" [51cm]) by the number of inches per pattern repeat.

20" (51cm) desired trim length / ½" (13mm) per shell repeat = 40 shells needed.

This calculation means you're going to make 40 pattern repeats—in this case, 40 shells, to achieve your desired length. If you don't end up with a whole number while doing this calculation, round up to the nearest whole number (you can always overlap the trim on the back side of your garment). So, how long does your foundation chain need to be to make 40 shells? Look at your swatch to see how many stitches you used per shell. If each of the shells is worked over 5 stitches, then

40 shells x 5 stitches each = 200 stitches in the foundation chain

Make sure this number corresponds with the suggested multiple indicated in the instructions—for instance, the directions might say "chain a multiple of 5 plus 1 stitches." This is because sometimes a pattern repeat starts in 1 stitch, then takes up 5 stitches to be completed. The next repeat actually starts in the last stitch of the first repeat, so you only need 5 more stitches (not 6) to make it—you already have your 'starter' stitch for the rest of the row. Therefore to make multiple repeats, you'd need to

chain a multiple of 5 plus 1 stitches

So in this case, add 1 more chain to the 200 chains in your foundation row to work the pattern correctly (always use the larger number when you're unsure). Work your foundation row of 201 chains and then work the pattern—your trim should be the perfect length.

A Failsafe Way to Avoid Coming Up Short

Although using math makes sense to determine the theoretical number of foundation chains you need, I always like to have a little insurance. If you're unsure about the number of chains to work, use the math to make an estimate, but then add a couple of extra chains to your foundation row. Add extra stitches in increments of the number needed to make a pattern repeat; this will allow you to make an extra shell or two at the end of the row if you need it.

If you're working with extra stitches, fasten off your yarn at the end of the foundation chain—this will make it easy to pull out any unnecessary chains later. Reattach the yarn at the beginning of the first row of stitches and work across. Repeat for the second row (if there is one). At this point you will have a good idea of the actual length of trim, so go ahead and measure it against your garment. If you are trimming a curved section, take the extra step of pinning the trim around the curve to make sure it fits. If the trim is too long, carefully unfasten the end of each row and pull out any extra stitches, starting with the last row worked. Secure the ends and continue to work the rest of your trim.

Even though using this insurance means you'll have a few extra ends to weave in, trust me, you'll be happy to see those extra stitches if you work a 201-chain foundation row and your trim ends up being half an inch too short. It's easier to pull out a few chains and weave in extra ends than it is to pull out your whole row and rework it from square one. And remember, you can also overlap any excess trim on the back side of the garment.

MOTIF MANIA: DO IT YOUR WAY

The motif-based projects in this book are meant as inspiration, so feel free to mix and match the motifs. If you like one motif more than another, you can make more of that motif. If you choose a garment with a different cut than the one shown in the project, or wear a larger or smaller size, you may need to make a different number of motifs than directed in the instructions. Or you might want to arrange them in a different way. Go for it! Just use your garment as a template—and make enough motifs to cover the desired area. Keep your garment nearby as you work, play with the arrangement

as you go, and continue to make motifs until you have enough of them to fill the space in a way that suits you.

CUSTOMIZE IT!

If you like the idea of a project, but it's not quite "you," don't be afraid to change the details! It's certainly fine to vary the yarn color, fiber, or brand. Just be sure to get something that you can work up to the same gauge. For many of these projects, gauge isn't even really an issue—a slightly larger flower on the Garden Party Cardigan (page 46), for instance, might be just your style. Feel free to leave out motifs you don't like, or search the stitch dictionary to find one you like better.

WAYS TO MAKE IT YOURS ▪ . ● . ●

- Change the size or shape of the embellished area by adding more motifs.
- Switch out the motifs used in the project for variations in the stitch dictionary.
- Play with color combinations—matching yarn is subtle; contrasting yarn will pop!
- Embellish your embellishment—small glass beads, sequins, shells, pailettes, and surface embroidery can transform the garment entirely.
- Try a different garment: Inset trims work well on skirts and dresses, too! Motifs can be applied to jeans and blazers as easily as tanks and tees.
- Change yarns—and not necessarily within the same weight category. Thicker yarns make chunky embellishments, while patterns worked in thread can be delicate and subtle.
- Start with a printed fabric or embroidered fabric, and try adding appliqués or readymade trims—the more layers in your look, the more crafty complexity to love.

Finishing

Okay, you've done all the crocheting and now it's time to move on to sewing. This might be a little scary if you've never sewn before, but if you can make a basic running stitch, you'll be fine.

PLACING YOUR DESIGN

Before you stitch anything, lay it out on the garment to see how it looks. Play with it: Move it around, stack it, or change the formation of the pieces until it looks right to you. If you have a dress form, place your prewashed garment on the dress form and pin the embellishments in place. A dress form will help you to deal with the three-dimensional aspects of the garment, but if you don't have one, try carefully pinning the embellishments to the garment while you are wearing it so that you can see what it looks like on and make any necessary adjustments. You can mark the placement of the motifs with tailor's chalk and remove the pins before removing the garment, or have a friend snap a photo for reference.

HAND-SEWING

Although I applied some of the trims in this book by machine, I found hand-sewing to be the easiest and most effective way to finish the pieces. Using the machine is tempting, but hand-sewing will give you the most control and is highly recommended, especially if you don't have a lot of sewing experience.

Applying Motifs

To secure motifs, use a running stitch along the outside edge of each motif. Work from the inside of the garment and use thread that coordinates with the motif (unless otherwise directed). Stitch around the outermost edge of each motif, making stitches in and out of the Vs of each stitch. For large motifs, in addition to the sewn outlines, add stitches in a large X shape across the center of each motif. Whenever possible, work your stitches from the inside of the garment and catch only the underside of the

crocheted stitches so the thread won't show. Gently tug the garment after every few stitches to loosen the stitches slightly and be sure the garment retains its ease. Knot your thread after sewing each motif so that if one thread happens to break, you won't have to re-sew all the motifs.

HOW TO KNOT YOUR THREAD

Tying knots in thread can be pesky, especially in tight spaces. Here's how to make it easy.

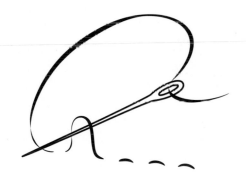

Stop sewing with 2–3" (5–7.5cm) of thread still on your needle. Bring the needle and thread to the inside of your garment. Make a very short stitch in the fabric and pull the thread through the stitch almost entirely, leaving a 1" (2.5cm) loop of thread. Bring the needle back through this loop twice and pull taut for a sturdy knot.

Applying Trims

Neckline, hemline, and sleeve trims are easy to add. For hem trims, pin the trim in place, making sure that the trim and garment edge overlap by at least ½" (13mm). Hand-sew a line of running stitches across the upper edge of the trim. Add a second row of stitches at the garment's bottom edge. For extra-wide trims, add a third row of stitching equidistant from the two lines of stitches you just made.

When working on the chain edge of a trim, move your needle in and out of the V shapes of the edge stitching for the most concealed yet secure stitching, as shown above.

MACHINE-SEWING

Using a sewing machine to apply embellishments is a bit tricky, and if you are a new sewer, or don't have a walking foot for your machine, my advice is to stick to hand-stitching. The results of hand-stitching really are worth it, since sometimes the short stitches produced by the machine can squeeze your crocheted stitches. It's also tough to sew exactly along curved lines when you're trying to manage a thick trim (a walking foot helps to alleviate this).

If you're an intermediate or advanced sewer, using a sewing machine will definitely shorten the time you spend attaching trims. Check specific project instructions to see if machine stitching is recommended.

To apply trim by machine, choose a thread that closely matches your yarn and load it into the machine. Change your foot to a walking foot, if possible. Pin the trim in place as desired, then position the garment under the foot with the trim on top so you can see what you are doing. Keep the excess trim width out of the feed dogs as much as possible.

Slide the trim and fabric under your walking foot so that the foot edge lines up with the trim edge. If your needle position is adjustable, move it as close to the straight edge of the trim as possible. Begin sewing slowly along the edge of the trim, removing the pins as you go. Remember to adjust your stitch length if necessary. Since the trim is probably thicker than most fabric, a longer stitch length will help the needle move along. Take care *not* to push the fabric and trim through your machine unless you find it absolutely necessary; let the machine grab and sew at its own pace for the best results. Remember to backstitch at the beginning and end of your trim, clip the threads, and you're done!

TIP: Test your machine with a swatch of trim and some scrap fabric before sewing directly onto your garment. If the machine is stubborn about moving over the crocheted trim, stick to hand-sewing for the best results.

CARING FOR YOUR EMBELLISHED GARMENTS

The safest way to take care of your finished projects is to dry clean them, since some yarns may shrink and pull at your garments in unexpected ways if you put them through the washing machine.

You may also hand-wash garments sparingly in cold water. Lay them flat to dry, and re-block them if necessary. Consider your yarn choice when you are making garments—a synthetic yarn is much less likely to shrink, and may be best for a garment you'll wash often. I've been able to get away with washing some embellished items on the cold setting in a front-loading washing machine, but I would never put them into a machine with an agitator, which is likely to stretch and tear embellishments. Never put embellished garments in the dryer, or the yarn and fabric might shrink in different proportions.

If you know you're not going to have the time to hand-wash or dry clean your items, make a gauge swatch with your yarn before you start a project and put it through the wash to see how it holds up. Acrylic and superwash wool yarns are made to be washable, and they may be just fine without any special care.

To store your embellished items, fold them and place them in a drawer. This will keep your stitches from stretching out of shape.

WORKING WITH STRETCH FABRICS ◦ . •

When working with stretch fabrics, such as a jersey T-shirt, you'll need to make sure you maintain the garment's stretch as you add embellishments. Here's why: If you have a stretchy garment and you sew something that doesn't stretch (the trim) on top of it, suddenly the garment won't stretch either. For this reason, always hand-sew embellishments to stretch fabrics. Hand-sewing will give you more control over stitch length and frequency. After every few stitches, tug on the working area slightly to put some ease back into the stitches. They may feel a little loose, but chances are good that when you're wearing the garment, you'll need the breathing room.

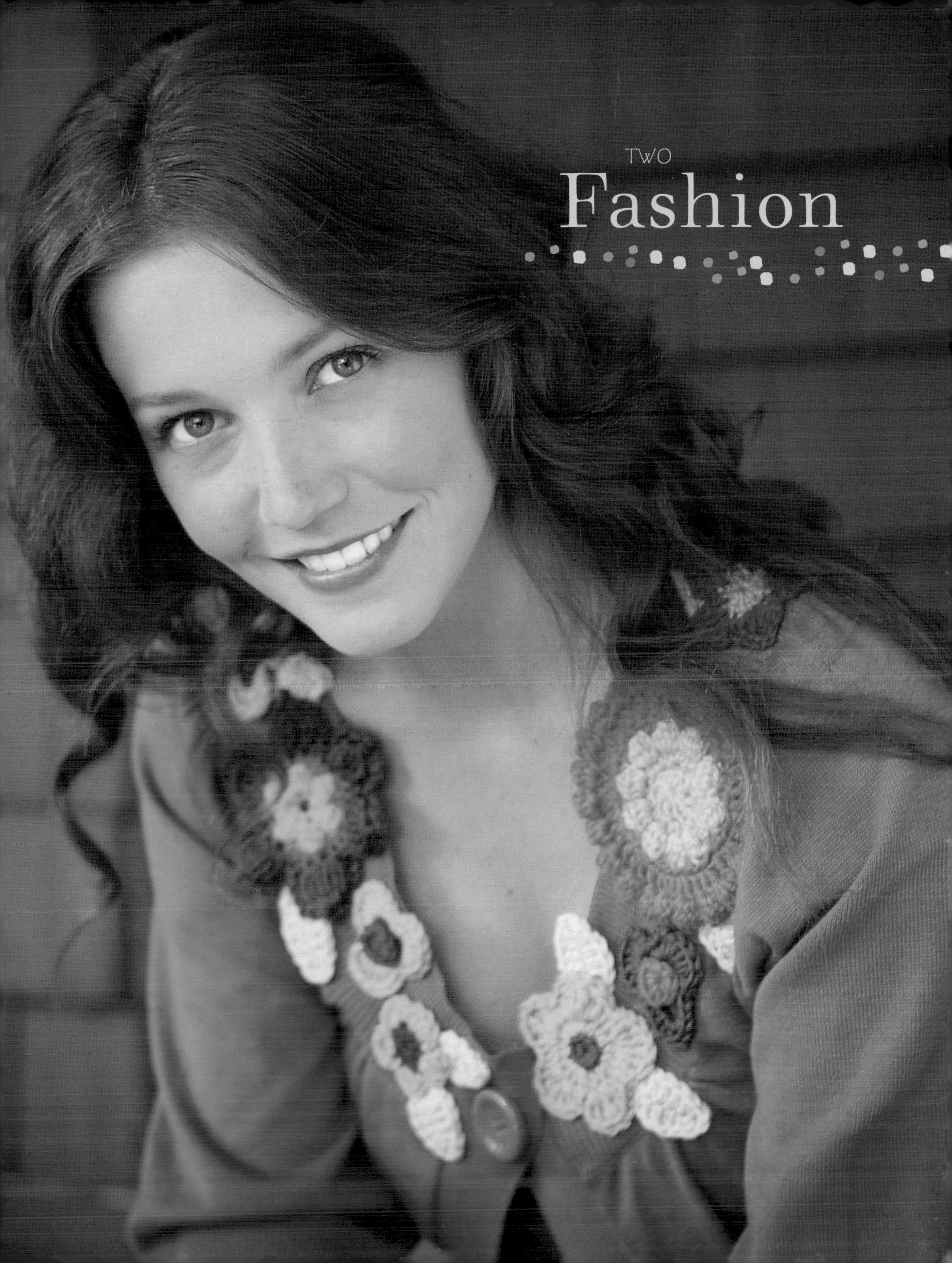

TWO

Fashion

Seaside Dress

This gently accented sundress glows with delicate inspiration. A sweet, simple trim works up as you go, making it easy to play with the looped design. You can follow any design you can draw with a line—tailor's chalk and fabric glue make this trim easy to apply, even when it follows twists and turns.

Skill Level Easy

Finished Measurements

Completed trim measures ⅜" (1cm) wide; the length of the trim is determined by your garment and placement design.

Materials

- 1 ball Coats and Clark *Aunt Lydia's Fashion Crochet Thread*, Size 3, 100% Mercerized Cotton, 150 yd (137m), #65 Warm Teal (1)
- Size B-1 (2.25mm) crochet hook, or size to obtain gauge
- Stitch marker
- Dress to embellish
- T-pins, iron, and blocking board
- Tailor's chalk
- Fabric glue
- Hand-sewing needle
- Sewing thread to match crochet thread

Gauge

Although gauge is not critical, you can make a gauge swatch by working 5 repeats of the pattern. The trim should measure ⅜" (1cm) wide and 2¾" (7cm) long.

Determining Trim Length

This trim gets longer with each row worked, so keep stitching until you achieve the correct length. You'll need one length of trim to match the collar edge measurement, and one length 12–20" (30.5–51cm) longer than the collar measurement for the looped trim. The added length gives you room to play with the design (you can pull out the extra stitches later if necessary).

Special Stitch

DOUBLE CROCHET 2 TOGETHER CLUSTER (dc2tog)

(Yo, insert hook in stitch, yo, draw yarn through stitch, yo, draw yarn through 2 lps on hook) twice in same stitch, yo, draw yarn through 3 lps on hook.

TRIM

> TIP: Mark the beginning cluster with a stitch marker so that it will be easy to find the starting end of the trim later.

ROW 1 (RS) Ch 5, dc2tog in 4th ch from hook, *ch 5, dc2tog in 4th ch from hook; repeat from * until trim measures desired length (see Notes on Determining Trim Length, left).

Fasten off. Weave in the ends (do not remove the stitch marker).

STITCH KEY
◯ = chain (ch)
⫮ = dc2tog

FINISHING

Block both lengths of trim and let them dry overnight.

Arrange the trims on your dress as desired. Once you've decided on a loop design, draw it directly onto the garment with tailor's chalk (available at sewing supply stores). Use this line as a guide when you glue the trim in place.

With the right side of the trim and the right side of the dress facing you, begin gluing the trim to the center back of your garment's collar, starting with the end of the trim that you marked with the stitch marker. Place small dots of glue on the back of the first three to four stitch clusters, then pinch them in place on the garment with your fingers. If the glue seeps, wipe away the excess with water while the glue is still wet.

Continue gluing all the way around the collar, stopping about four clusters before you meet the beginning of the trim. If your trim is too long, cut it about four clusters longer than you want it to be and pull out the extra stitches. Fasten off the yarn and weave in the end, then finish gluing the trim in place. Apply the second length of trim in the same manner, following the line you drew with the tailor's chalk. Allow the glue to dry for 24 hours, then hand-sew each length of trim securely in place.

Breezy Tunic

Add a little flash to your summer wardrobe with peek-a-boo sleeves. An inset trim along the length of each sleeve makes a roomy top perfect for warm summer days. You'll need some sewing reconstruction skills for this project, so be sure to pay attention when you take apart the sleeves.

Skill Level Intermediate

Finished Measurements

Trim measures 2" (5cm) wide, trim length is determined by your garment.

Materials

- 1 skein of Fiesta Yarns *La Luz Multi*, 100% mulberry silk, 210 yd (192m), 2 oz (57g) in #17132 Tequila Sunrise (2)
- Size D-3 (3.25mm) crochet hook, or size to obtain gauge
- T-pins, iron, and blocking board
- Cotton tunic with ¾-length sleeves to embellish
- Seam ripper
- 1 yd (.9m) coordinating double-fold bias tape (if tunic does not have finished sleeves)
- Sewing machine (optional)
- Hand-sewing needle
- Sewing thread to match yarn and tunic
- Straight pins

Gauge

One flower measures 2" (5cm) in diameter. Make an even number of flowers to match the garment's sleeve length. If your sleeve length is not a multiple of 2" (5cm), make the trim slightly shorter than the existing sleeve.

Making Trim

This trim consists of connected flower motifs. Make and connect the motifs as you go, referring to the diagram to see how to join each successive flower, then crochet around the edge as directed. Make one length of trim for each sleeve.

Special Stitches

2 TREBLE CLUSTER (2-tr cluster) (Yo twice, insert hook in stitch, yo, draw yarn through stitch, [yo, draw yarn through 2 lps on hook] twice) twice in same stitch, yo, draw yarn through 3 lps on hook.
PICOT Ch 3, sc in 3rd ch from hook.

FLOWER 1

Ch 8, join with a sl st to form a ring.
ROUND 1 (RS) Ch 1, *sc in ring, ch 5, 2-tr cluster in ring, picot, ch 5; repeat from * 4 times, sl st in first sc to join—5 clusters.

FLOWER 2

Ch 8, join with a sl st to form a ring.
ROUND 1 (RS) Ch 1, *sc in ring, ch 5, 2-tr cluster in ring, ch 1, sl st in any picot on flower 1, ch 1, sc in 2nd ch from hook, ch 5; repeat from * once, **sc in ring, ch 5, 2-tr cluster in ring, picot, ch 5; repeat from ** twice, sl st in first sc to join—5 clusters. Fasten off.

FLOWER 3

Work same as Flower 2, joining to only *one* petal (the one opposite of the joined petals) on the previous flower. Fasten off.

Repeat Flowers 2 and 3 until trim measures same as sleeve length, working an even number of flowers total. Refer to the diagram for placement—the fourth flower will be joined at two petals, the fifth at one, the sixth at two, and so on. Fasten off. Weave in all ends.

Edging

ROUND 1 (RS) With right side facing, join yarn to center picot on short edge on flower 1 (refer to the diagram), ch 7, sc in next petal, *ch 5, tr in junction between 2 flower petals, ch 5, sc in next petal picot**, ch 5, tr in 4th ch of the next petal on the same flower, tr in 2nd ch of next flower petal, ch 5, sc in next petal picot*; repeat from * to * across, ending last repeat at ** on last flower, ch 7, sc in end petal picot, ch 7, sc in next petal picot; repeat from * to * across, ending last repeat at ** on last petal, ch 7, sc in first petal picot. Fasten off.

End Trim

ROW 1 (RS) With right side facing, join yarn in 5th ch to the right of last sc in Edging, ch 1, sc in same stitch, sc in each of next 4 ch, sc in each of next 5 ch of next lp. Fasten off.

Repeat end trim across other short edge of trim.

ATTACHING TRIM TO TUNIC

Pin the trim to your blocking board, squaring off the corners with T-pins. Block the trim and let it dry.

With a seam ripper, carefully remove the sleeves of your tunic at the shoulder. If your sleeve has a bias binding on the sleeve edge, remove it as well and set it aside. Cut straight down the length of the sleeve from the center of the shoulder to the center of the sleeve's bottom edge. Press each cut edge under ½" (13mm). Turn the ½" (13mm) fold under halfway, ¼" (6mm), and press again. Using a sewing machine (optional), sew along the pressed edge of the sleeve. Repeat for the other edge, then repeat the entire process with the second sleeve.

Line up the short edge of the trim with the shoulder and the long edges with the sewn sleeve edges. Carefully hand-sew the trim in place along the sewn sleeve edges. Sew in and out of the V of each chain stitch to conceal the thread.

Reinsert the sleeve into the shirt shoulder and pin it in place. The sleeve will have a slightly larger circumference due to the added width of the trim, so gather it slightly to fit. Use the existing shoulder seam as a guide to re-pin the sleeve in place, and machine or hand-sew it in place.

If necessary, trim the bottom of your sleeve to match the length of the trim. Cut a piece of bias tape 1" (2.5cm) longer than the circumference of the sleeve. Unfold the tape completely and fold it in half with short ends matching and right sides facing. Stitch ½" (13mm) in from the raw short edge, then cut off ¼" (6mm) of excess tape. Examine your bias tape and notice that there is one narrow fold and one wide fold. Next, slide the tape ring over the outside of the sleeve, lining up the raw edge of the narrow fold with the bottom edge of the sleeve. Pin the tape in place around the edge and stitch around the tape, close to the raw edge. Fold the tape over the sleeve hem and under to the inside of the shirt; refold the wide fold so that the raw edge is encased on the inside of the sleeve. On the right side of the shirt, sew around the top fold of the bias tape, encasing the sleeve edge, trim, and inside fold of the bias tape. Repeat for the second sleeve.

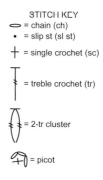

STITCH KEY
◠ = chain (ch)
• = slip st (sl st)
+ = single crochet (sc)
╫ = treble crochet (tr)
⬮ = 2-tr cluster
⬮ = picot

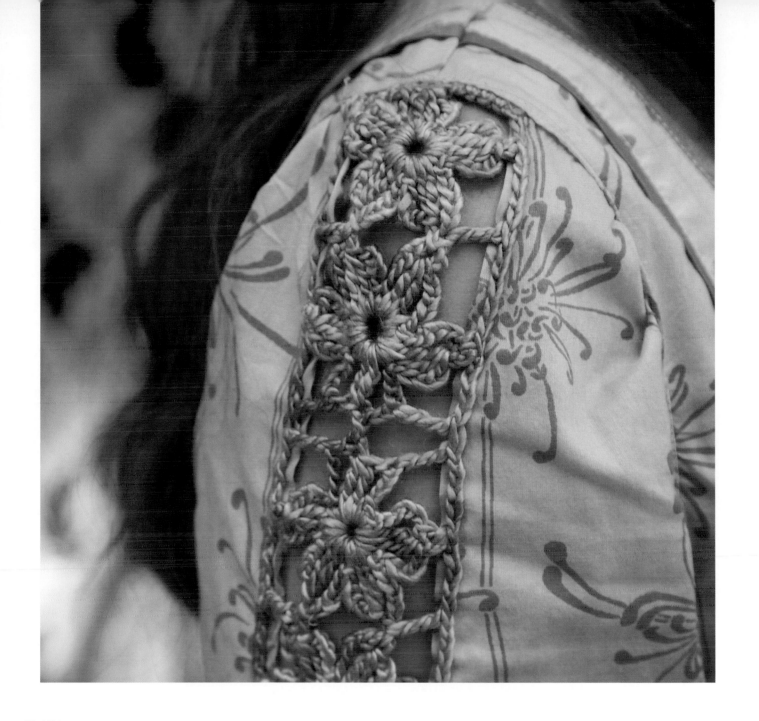

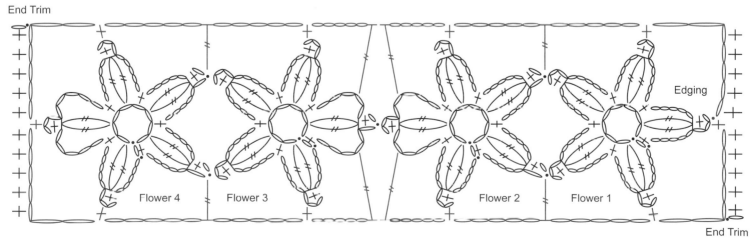

End Trim

Flower 4   Flower 3   Flower 2   Flower 1

Edging

End Trim

Garden Party Cardigan

Bold flowers turn a basic cardigan into a statement piece, and a rainbow of available yarn colors means you can customize any sweater to suit your fancy. This project is also the perfect fix for favorite sweaters with holes or stains—just use the flowers to cover the flaws. If you're not keen on stitching up a whole garden, crochet only your favorite flower and finish it off with a pin-back, that way it can "grow" anywhere you like!

Skill Level Easy

Finished Measurements

Smallest flower (5-Petal Flower) measures 1¾" (4.5cm) in diameter, largest flower (Bobble Poppy) measures 4" (10cm) in diameter.

Materials

- 1 skein each of Cascade Yarns *Superwash 220*, 100% superwash wool, 220 yd (201m), 3½ oz (100g), in #825 orange (A), #826 peach (B), #907 dark orange (C), #908 magenta (D), #809 red (E), #838 pink (F), and #860 light green (G) ⬤③
- Size F-5 (3.75mm) crochet hook, or size to obtain gauge
- Yarn needle
- T-pins, iron, and blocking board (optional)
- Cardigan to embellish
- Straight pins
- Hand-sewing needle
- Sewing thread to match cardigan

Gauge

Although gauge is not critical for this project, refer to the finished measurements for final motif sizes to check your gauge.

Special Stitches

DOUBLE CROCHET 4 TOGETHER (bobble) (Yo, insert hook in stitch, yo, draw yarn through stitch, yo, draw yarn through 2 lps on hook) 4 times in same stitch, yo, draw yarn through 5 lps on hook.

TREBLE 6 TOGETHER CLUSTER (tr6tog) (Yo twice, insert hook in stitch, yo, draw yarn through stitch, [yo, draw yarn through 2 lps on hook] twice) 3 times in same stitch, (yo twice, insert hook in next stitch, yo, draw yarn through stitch, [yo, draw yarn through 2 lps on hook] twice) 3 times in same stitch, yo, draw yarn through all 7 lps on hook.

BOBBLE POPPY (MAKE 1)

With yarn B, make a magic ring.

ROUND 1 (RS) Ch 3 (counts as first dc throughout), 9 dc in ring, sl st in top of beginning ch to join—10 dc.

ROUND 2 (RS) Ch 2 (counts as first hdc throughout), hdc in first stitch, 2 hdc in each dc around, sl st in top of beginning ch to join, turn—20 hdc.

ROUND 3 (WS) With wrong side facing, ch 1, sc in first stitch, bobble in next hdc, *sc in next hdc, bobble in next hdc; repeat from * around, sl st in top of beginning ch to join—20 stitches. Fasten off B.

ROUND 4 (WS) With wrong side facing, join C in any sc, ch 2, hdc in first stitch, *hdc in next stitch, 2 hdc in next stitch; repeat from * around, sl st in top of beginning ch to join, turn—30 hdc.

ROUND 5 (RS) With right side facing, ch 3, dc in next hdc, 2 dc in next hdc, *dc in next 2 hdc, 2 dc in next hdc; repeat from * around, sl st in top of beginning ch to join, turn—40 dc.

ROUND 6 (WS) With wrong side facing, ch 1, sc in first stitch, bobble in next dc, *sc in next dc, bobble in next dc;

repeat from * around, sl st in top of beginning ch to join—40 stitches.

Fasten off. Weave in the ends.

6-PETAL FLOWER (MAKE 1)

With yarn A, make a magic ring.

ROUND 1 (WS) Ch 1, 6 sc in ring, sl st in first sc to join—6 sc.

ROUND 2 (WS) Ch 1, (sc, bobble) in each sc around, sl st in first sc to join, turn—12 stitches. Fasten off A.

ROUND 3 (RS) With right side facing, join yarn C in first sc of round 2, ch 2, hdc in first stitch, *hdc in next stitch, 2 hdc in next stitch; repeat from * around, ending with hdc in last stitch, sl st in top of beginning ch to join—18 hdc. Fasten off C.

ROUND 4 (RS) With right side facing, join yarn D in beginning ch in Round 3, ch 1, *sc in next hdc, ch 5, tr6tog over next 2 hdc (3 tr in each stitch), ch 2, sl st in top of tr6tog for picot, ch 5; repeat from * around, sl st in first sc to join—12 ch-5 lps; 6 clusters.

Fasten off. Weave in the ends.

EGG FLOWER (MAKE 1)

With yarn E, make a magic ring.

ROUND 1 (RS) Ch 2, 9 hdc in ring, sl st in top of beginning ch to join—10 hdc. Fasten off A.

ROUND 2 With right side facing, join F in beginning chain of Round 1, ch 2, hdc in BL of first stitch, 2 hdc in BL of each hdc around, sl st

in top of beginning ch to join—20 hdc.

ROUND 3 Ch 2, (dc, 2 tr) in next hdc, (2 tr, dc) in next hdc, hdc in next hdc, *hdc in next hdc, (dc, 2 tr) in next hdc, (2 tr, dc) in next hdc, hdc in next hdc; repeat from * around, sl st in top of beginning ch to join—40 stitches.

Fasten off. Weave in the ends.

3-PETAL FLOWER (MAKE 1 IN EACH OF THE FOLLOWING COLOR COMBINATIONS: A/D, E/F, AND D/C)

With first color, make a magic ring.

ROUND 1 (RS) Ch 1, (sc, ch 5) 3 times in ring, sl st in first sc to join—3 ch-5 lps.

ROUND 2 Ch 1, (sc, hdc, 6 dc, hdc, sc) in each ch-5 lp around, sl st in first sc to join—30 stitches.

Fasten off. Weave in the ends.

Flower Center

With 2nd color, make a magic ring.

ROUND 1 (RS) Ch 2, 9 hdc in ring, sl st in top of beginning ch to join—10 hdc.

Fasten off, leaving a tail for sewing.

With the yarn tail, sew the flower center on top of the 3-petal piece, making running stitches around the single crochets of Round 1 to secure the center. Weave in the ends.

5-PETAL FLOWER (MAKE 1 IN EACH OF THE FOLLOWING COLOR COMBINATIONS: B/F, E/A)

With first color, make a magic ring.

ROUND 1 (RS) Ch 3 (counts as first dc), 9 dc in ring, sl st in top of beginning ch to join—10 dc. Fasten off first color.

ROUND 2 With right side facing, join 2nd color in beginning ch in Round 1, *ch 1, 3 dc in next dc, ch 1, sl st in next dc; repeat from * around—5 petals.

Fasten off. Weave in the ends.

5-PETAL POINTY FLOWER (MAKE 1)

With yarn F, make a magic ring.

ROUND 1 (RS) Ch 3 (counts as dc), 9 dc in ring, join—10 dc. Fasten off F.

ROUND 2 With right side facing, join E in beginning ch of Round 1, *ch 1, (2 dc, ch 2, 2 dc) in next dc, ch 1, sl st in next stitch; repeat from * around, ending last repeat with sl st to join—5 petals.

Fasten off. Weave in the ends.

SMALL LEAF (MAKE 8)

Ch 8.

ROUND 1 (RS) Sc in 2nd ch from hook, hdc in next ch, dc in next 3 ch, hdc in next ch, (sc, ch 1, sc) in last ch, working across opposite side of foundation ch, hdc in next ch, dc in next 3 ch, hdc in next ch, sc in next ch, ch 1, sl st in first sc to join—16 stitches.

Fasten off. Weave in the ends.

FINISHING

Block the flowers (optional).

Pin the crocheted flowers to your cardigan as shown in the photograph or as desired. With a hand-sewing needle and thread to match the sweater, sew the flowers to the cardigan from the inside of the sweater, being careful to catch only the underside of the crochet stitches (so the thread won't show through).

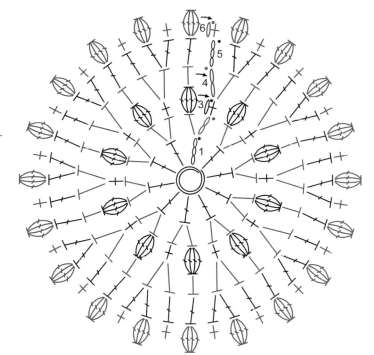

Bobble Poppy

6-Petal Flower

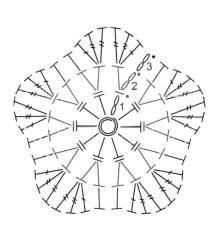

Egg Flower

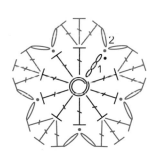

5-Petal Flower

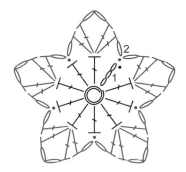

5-Petal Pointy Flower

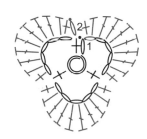

3-Petal Flower

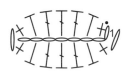

Small Leaf

Modern Harlequin Dress

Add some personality to your little black dress with a colorful collar and hem design. Choose your favorite color combinations—the design is completely up to you. Any sport-weight yarn will work, so check your stash before you spend any cash. You can also use this or any wide trim as a secret way to raise a neckline or lower a hem—just be sure that at least ½" (13mm) of the trim overlaps with the garment.

Skill Level Easy

Finished Size

As written, the collar trim measures 2" (5cm) wide and the hem trim measures 2¼" (5.5cm) wide. You can vary both the length and the width of the trim by changing the number of shells across and the number of rows worked, respectively.

Materials

* 1 ball GGH *Wollywasch*, 100% wool, 138 yd (125m), 1¾ oz (50g), #81 yellow, #97 pale pink, #98 bright pink, #173 olive, #145 orange, #156 off white, and #165 purple ②
* Size D-3 (3.25mm) crochet hook, or size to obtain gauge
* Measuring tape
* Dress with round collar to embellish
* Yarn needle
* T-pins, iron, and blocking board
* Straight pins
* Hand-sewing needle
* Sewing thread to match yarn

Gauge

18 stitches (3 shells) by 3 rows of shells measures 3" (7.5cm) long by 1" (2.5cm) wide.

Determining Trim Length

Measure the circumference of both the collar and hemline of your garment and round the numbers to the nearest whole inch. Refer to *Determining Foundation Chain Length* (page 33) for instructions on how to determine the number of chains in the foundation chain for your collar and hem trim lengths.

Color Sequences

COLLAR	HEM
A pale pink	A olive
B yellow	B purple
C purple	C pale pink
D off white	D orange
E bright pink	E off white
F olive	F bright pink
	G yellow

TRIM

With yarn A, ch a multiple of 6 stitches plus 2.

ROW 1 (RS) Sl st in 2nd ch from hook, *sk next 2 ch, 5 dc in next ch (shell made), sk next 2 ch, sl st in next ch; repeat from * across, fasten off.

ROW 2 With RS facing, attach yarn B at the beginning of previous row. Ch 3 (counts as dc), work 2 dc in first stitch (half shell completed), *sk next 2 dc, sl st in next dc, sk next 2 dc, 5 dc in next sl st; repeat from * across, ending last repeat with 3 dc in last sl st (half shell), fasten off.

ROW 3 With RS facing, attach yarn C at the beginning of previous row. Ch 1, sl st in first dc, *sk next 2 dc, 5 dc in

next sl st, sk next 2 dc, sl st in next dc; repeat from *, ending last repeat with sl st in top of last dc.

Repeat Rows 2 and 3 alternating colors on each row with yarns D, E, and F for collar, and once more with yarn G for hem.

FINISHING

Block both lengths of trim and let them dry. If the trim is too long for your blocking board, block it in sections.

Fold the collar trim in half to find the center, then pin the center point to the center front of the collar. Pin the left and right edges of the trim to the center back of the collar. Next, place more pins around the trim, distributing it evenly over the collar. Make sure the trim overlaps with the garment by at least ½" (13mm). Hand-sew the trim in place by making two lines around the

collar—one around the top of the collar, and one around the bottom of the trim. Try to catch only the underside of the trim as you sew. If you are working with a knit dress or tee, be sure to stitch loosely in order to maintain the ease of the knit material. This will allow the garment to stretch when necessary (for instance, when you're putting it on). Attach the trim to the hemline in the same manner.

STITCH KEY

⬭ = chain (ch)

• = slip st (sl st)

T = double crochet (dc)

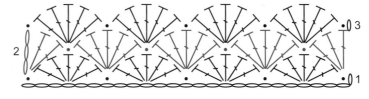

Patchwork Pullover

This colorful embellished shirt is sure to be a conversation starter, and the quilt-like stars are surprisingly simple to make. Crocheting in the space between each stitch, rather than under the V, gives these circles their star-shaped centers.

Skill Level Easy

Finished Size

Each circle motif measures 1⅜" (3.5cm) in diameter, and each half circle measures ¾" (2cm) across. Using your shirt as a template, make as many circles as you need to fill the desired space.

Materials

- 1 skein of GGH *Bali*, 50% cotton, 50% acrylic, 158 yd (145m), 1¾ oz (50g), in #03 white (A), #78 green (B), and #40 blue (C) ⓷
- Size F-5 (3.75mm) crochet hook or size needed to obtain gauge
- Shirt to embellish (look for a knit pullover with gathering just under the collar)
- Yarn needle
- Hand-sewing needle
- Sewing thread to match yarns

Gauge

Circle motif measures 1⅜" (3.5cm) in diameter; half circle measures ¾" (2cm) across.

NOTE: *Color combinations and motif counts are based on a size small shirt. Start by making the motifs listed, then, using your shirt as a template, make more full and half-circle motifs to fill the space.*

CIRCLE (MAKE 35: 5 OF COLOR COMBINATION A/B, 6 EACH OF A/C, B/A, B/C, 5 OF C/A, AND 7 OF C/B)

With first color, make a magic ring.

ROUND 1 (RS) Ch 3 (counts as first dc), 9 dc in ring—10 dc.

ROUND 2 With RS facing, attach second color in the space between first 2 dc, ch 1, 2 sc in same space, *2 sc in space between next 2 dc; repeat from * around, sl st in first sc to join—20 sc.

Fasten off and leave a long tail for sewing. Weave in all of the center ends.

HALF CIRCLE (MAKE 2, 1 IN EACH COMBINATION: B/A, C/A)

With first color, make a magic ring.

ROUND 1 (RS) Ch 3 (counts as first dc), 5 dc in ring—6 dc.

ROUND 2 With RS facing, attach second color in space between beginning ch and first dc, ch 1, 2 sc in same space, *2 sc in space between next 2 dc; repeat from * three times—10 sc.

Fasten off and leave a long tail for sewing. Weave in all of the center ends.

ASSEMBLY

Using your shirt as a guide, arrange the motifs as desired along the yoke of the shirt. Stagger the circles so that one row of circles nests in the space between the circles of the previous row, placing half circles at the left and right ends of the circle rows as necessary where the yoke meets the sleeve (the project pictured on page 53 uses two half circles, one near each sleeve seam). Using the long yarn tails, sew all of the motifs together, one at a time, being sure to mimic the shape of the shirt. Hand-sew the circle panel to the shirt from the inside of the shirt. Use a running stitch and insert the needle through the back side of the crochet work only so that the sewn stitches are invisible.

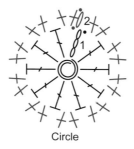

Circle

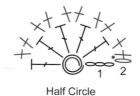

Half Circle

STITCH KEY

⬮ = chain (ch)

• = slip st (sl st)

✛ = single crochet (sc)

┬ = double crochet (dc)

◎ = magic ring

Fuzzy Bib Top

This flowering bib is a great way to add some style to your favorite tee. Make it with the recommended super-fine mohair for softened, fuzzy motifs, or try crochet thread for a delicate design. Remember to experiment with your yarn choices—a textured yarn will give your garments a completely different look and appeal.

Finished Size

Bib measures 5½" (14cm) wide by 6¾" (17cm) long.

Materials

- 1 skein each of GGH *Soft-Kid*, 70% super kid mohair, 5% wool, 25% polyamide, 151 yd (138m), 1⅖ oz (40g), #001 white (A) and #062 orange (B) ⓵
- Size D-3 (3.25mm) crochet hook, or size to obtain gauge
- Scoop-neck T-shirt to embellish
- T-pins, iron, and blocking board
- Straight pins
- Hand-sewing needle and
- Sewing thread to match yarn

Gauge

One flower motif is 2" (5cm) in diameter.

FLOWER MOTIF (MAKE 6)

With yarn A, ch 6, join with a sl st to form a ring.

ROUND 1 (RS) Ch 1, 12 sc in ring, sl st in first sc to join—12 sc.

ROUND 2 With right side facing, join B in any sc, ch 3, (tr, ch 3, sl st) in next sc, *sl st in next sc, ch 3, (tr, ch 3, sl st) in next sc; repeat from * four times more, sl st in first sl st to join—6 petals.

ROUND 3 With right side facing, join A in tr of any petal, ch 1, sc in tr, *ch 4, sc in tr of next petal; repeat from * around, ending with ch 4, sl st in first sc to join—6 ch-4 lps.

ROUND 4 *(Ch 1, hdc, dc, hdc, ch 1, sl st, ch 1, hdc, dc, hdc, ch 1) in next ch-4 lp, sl st in next sc; repeat from * around, sl st in first sl st to join—12 petals.

Fasten off, leaving a long tail for sewing motifs together.

SMALL FLOWER MOTIF (MAKE 2)

Work the same as Flower Motif through Round 3. Fasten off, leaving a long tail for sewing motifs together.

ASSEMBLING BIB

Sew six flower motifs together as shown in diagram. Sew one small flower motif over the two center holes created by the motifs (see shaded area on diagram). Weave in the ends.

EDGING

ROUND 1 (RS) With right side facing, starting at the top left corner, join B in center dc of 4th petal to the left of the center seam (see diagram), ch 1, sc in same dc, ch 5 (corner), sc in next dc, ch 3, sc in next dc, *(ch 3, dc) in each of next 2 dc, (ch 3, sc) in each of next 2 dc*; repeat from * to * once, **(ch 3, sc) in each of next 3 dc**, repeat from * to * once; repeat from ** to ** once; repeat from * to * twice; ch 5, sc in next dc (corner), (ch 3, sc) in each of next 2 dc; repeat from * to * once, ch 3, sl st in first sc to join—34 ch-3 lps; 2 ch-5 lps.

Work now progresses in rows.

ROW 2 Sl st to 3rd ch of first ch-5 lp, ch 1, 4 sc in first ch-5 lp, 4 sc in each ch-3 sp across left side, bib bottom and right side to ch-5 corner lp, 4 sc in ch-5 lp—116 sc. Fasten off.

ROW 3 With right side facing, join A in first sc of top left corner, ch 1, sc in first sc, *ch 6, sk 3 sc, sc in next sc; repeat from * across, ending with sc in last sc—29 ch-6 lps. Fasten off.

Top Edge

With right side facing, join A to center ch of last ch-6 lp in Row 3 of edging, ch 3 (counts as dc), dc in each of next 2 ch, dc in each stitch across top edge, ending with dc in each of next 3 ch of last ch-6 lp in Row 3 of edging—43 dc.

Fasten off. Weave in all of the yarn ends.

BLOCKING

Trace the collar line of the shirt you are embellishing on a clean piece of paper and cut the paper along the line, discard the top portion of the paper. Fold the bottom section of the paper in half to determine the collar's center, and mark it with a pencil. Pin the paper collar down to your blocking board. Place the crocheted piece over the paper collar and line up the bib's center with the paper center. Pin the bib in place, stretching the top of the bib slightly to match the top edge of the paper collar template. Block the collar and let it dry.

FINISHING

Pin the bib to your shirt. With thread that coordinates with each yarn, hand-sew across the top of the bib and around the "U" shape of the bib. Tug the tee every few stitches to loosen the stitches slightly (to retain its stretch). Leave the outer loops of the edging loose, or hand-sew them in place, if desired.

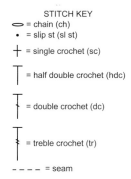

STITCH KEY
= chain (ch)
= slip st (sl st)
= single crochet (sc)
= half double crochet (hdc)
= double crochet (dc)
= treble crochet (tr)
- - - - = seam

TOP EDGE

EDGING

JOINING OF
SECOND AND
SUCCESSIVE
FLOWER MOTIFS

E3 E2 E1 4

Scalloped Spring Jacket

This super-simple trim packs a visual punch perfect for a fun floral jacket. For a romantic look, try using this trim pattern with a smaller gauge yarn on a plain jacket—the thinner yarn will produce tiny scallops that dance along the jacket edge. This trim would also be sweet peeking out from the hem of a skirt.

Skill Level Beginner

Finished Measurements

Completed trim measures ¾" (2cm) wide; the length of the trim is determined by your garment.

Materials

- 1 skein of Berocco *Comfort*, 50% nylon, 50% acrylic, 210 yds (193m), 3½ oz (100g), in #9723 Rosebud ④
- Size H-8 (5mm) crochet hook
- Measuring tape
- Coat to embellish
- T-pins, iron, and blocking board
- Straight pins
- Sewing machine or hand-sewing needle
- Sewing thread to match jacket

Gauge

To make a gauge swatch, chain 20 and work as directed in the pattern. The swatch should measure approximately 4" (10cm) in length and contain 3 scallops.

Notes on Measuring the Coat for the Trim

Measure all of the areas on the coat that you'd like to accent with trim, such as the collar, front flap, sleeve edges, and hem. Make a separate length of trim for each section. You'll also need to make a separate piece of trim for the collar and the front placket so that the trim sections will both face right side out. Decide which areas you'd like to trim, then measure and record the length of each section.

Refer to *Determining Foundation Chain Length* (page 33) for instructions on how to determine number of chains in the foundation chain for each length of trim.

STITCH KEY
⌒ = chain (ch)
• = slip st (sl st)
+ = single crochet (sc)
╥ = double crochet (dc)

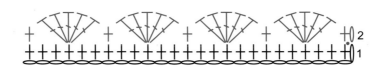

SCALLOP TRIM (MAKE 1 PIECE FOR EACH TRIMMED SECTION)

Ch a multiple of 6 stitches plus 2.

ROW 1 (RS) Sc in 2nd ch from hook, sc in each ch across. Fasten off.

ROW 2 With right side facing, join yarn in first sc, ch 1, sc in first sc, *sk next 2 sc, 5 dc in next sc (shell made), sk next 2 sc, sc in next sc; repeat from * across.

Fasten off. Weave in the ends.

FINISHING

Block the trim (optional) and allow it to dry. Pin the trim to the underside of the coat collar, placket, sleeves, hem, and any other desired areas. Place the trim so that only the scallops peek out and the single crochet row is concealed by the coat edge. Machine or hand-sew the trim in place with coordinating thread.

Floral Motif Yoke Top

This motif-based top is the perfect fit for summer. Easy sewing tricks make it simple to attach the yoke to a bit of your favorite fabric for a 100 percent handmade top, or use the alternative instructions to refashion a store-bought tank.

Skill Level Advanced

Finished Size

Crocheted bodice measures 13" (33cm) wide by 18" (46cm) in length. Fabric bottom fits loosely and is sized for Small (Medium, Large). Measurements are 42 (46, 50)" (107 [117, 127]cm) around by 17 (19, 21)" (43 [48, 53.5]cm) long, or use an oversized store-bought tank top.

Materials

- 2 skeins of Tahki Stacy Charles *Cotton Classic*, 100% mercerized cotton, 108 yd (100m), 1¾ oz (50g), in #3774 Pine Green 🔳
- Size F-5 (3.75mm) crochet hook or size to obtain gauge
- T-pins, iron, and blocking board
- 1 (1¼, 1¼) yd (.92 [1.14, 1.14]m) 45"- (114.5cm) wide prewashed cotton fabric *or* loose-fitting tank top
- Scissors
- Water-soluble fabric marker
- 1 package ¼"- (6mm) wide double-fold bias tape
- Sewing machine
- Straight pins
- Pinking shears (optional)
- Hand-sewing needle
- Sewing threads to match fabric and yarn
- One ¾" (2cm) diameter button

Gauge

One completed Flower Motif measures 3" (7.5cm) by 3" (7.5cm); 20 dc worked over 9 rows measures 4" (10cm).

Special Stitches

DOUBLE CROCHET 2 TOGETHER DECREASE (dc2tog) (Yo, insert hook in next stitch, yo, draw yarn through stitch, yo, draw yarn through 2 lps on hook) twice, yo, draw yarn through 3 lps on hook.

TREBLE 3 TOGETHER CLUSTER (tr3tog) (Yo twice, insert hook in stitch, yo, draw yarn through stitch, [yo, draw yarn through 2 lps on hook] twice) 3 times in same stitch, yo, draw yarn through 4 lps on hook.

TREBLE 4 TOGETHER CLUSTER (tr4tog) (Yo twice, insert hook in stitch, yo, draw yarn through stitch, [yo, draw yarn through 2 lps on hook] twice) 4 times in same stitch, yo, draw yarn through 5 lps on hook.

FLOWER MOTIF (MAKE 8)

Ch 6, join with a sl st to form a ring.
ROUND 1 (RS) Ch 4, tr3tog in ring (counts as tr4tog), ch 4, (tr4tog, ch 4) 5 times in ring, sl st in first tr4tog cluster to join—6 clusters; 6 ch-4 lps.
ROUND 2 Ch 1, sc in first cluster, ch 4, sc in next ch-4 lp, *ch 4, sc in next cluster, ch 4, sc in next ch-4 lp; repeat from * around, ending with ch 2, hdc in first sc to join instead of last ch-4 lp—12 ch-4 loops.
ROUND 3 Ch 1, sc in first lp, *ch 2, (2 dc, ch 2, 2 dc) in next ch-4 lp, (ch 2, sc) in each of next 2 ch-4 lps; repeat from * around, omitting last sc, sl st in first sc to join—16 ch-2 sps. Fasten off. Weave in all ends.

Block all eight motifs to measure 3" (7.5cm) by 3" (7.5cm).

FRONT PANEL

The front panel is made of four flower motifs placed side by side. With right sides facing, line up the edges of two motifs and, working on one edge, join the motifs using a slip stitch through the back loops only (14 sl st). Join two more motifs to make the four-motif-wide panel.

Front Top Edging

ROW 1 (RS) With right side facing, join yarn at the top right corner of the four-motif panel, ch 3 (counts as dc throughout), dc in each stitch across entire panel, turn and continue with Right Strap—56 dc.

Right Strap

ROW 1 (WS) Ch 3, dc in next 11 dc, turn—12 dc.
ROW 2 (RS) Ch 3, dc in each stitch across, turn—12 dc.
ROW 3 (WS) Ch 3, dc in next 8 dc, (dc2tog in next 2 dc) twice, turn—10 stitches.
ROW 4 (RS) Ch 3, dc in each stitch across, turn—10 dc.
ROWS 5–22 Repeat row 4.
ROW 23 (WS) Ch 3, dc in next 7 dc, 2 dc in each of next 2 dc, turn—12 dc.
ROW 24 (RS) Ch 3, dc in each stitch across, turn—12 dc.

Fasten off. Weave in the ends.

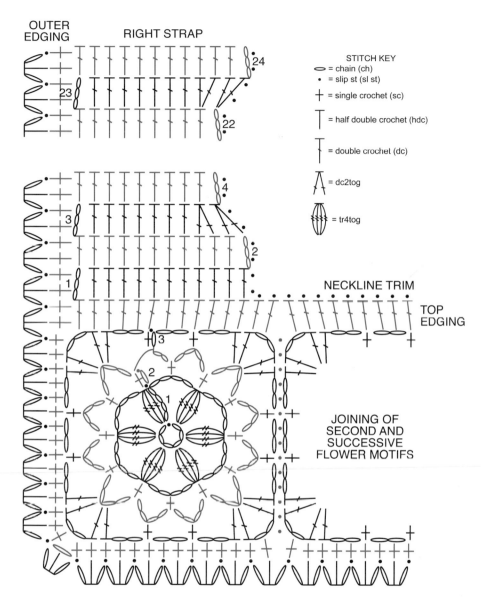

OUTER EDGING

RIGHT STRAP

24
23
22
4
3
2
1

STITCH KEY

- ⌒ = chain (ch)
- • = slip st (sl st)
- + = single crochet (sc)
- Τ = half double crochet (hdc)
- Ƭ = double crochet (dc)
- Λ = dc2tog
- ⬮ = tr4tog

NECKLINE TRIM

TOP EDGING

3
2
1

JOINING OF SECOND AND SUCCESSIVE FLOWER MOTIFS

Left Strap

With wrong side facing, sk 32 stitches to the left of last stitch made in Row 1 of Right Strap, join yarn in next dc (12 stitches to the right of the left edge).

ROW 1 (WS) Ch 3, dc in each of next 11 dc, turn—12 dc.

ROW 2 (RS) Ch 3, dc in each stitch across, turn—12 dc.

ROW 3 (WS) Ch 3, (dc2tog in next 2 dc) twice, dc in each stitch across, turn—10 dc.

ROW 4 (RS) Ch 3, dc in each stitch across, turn—10 dc.

ROWS 5–22 Repeat row 4.

ROW 23 (WS) Ch 3, 2 dc in each of next 2 dc, dc in each stitch across, turn—12 dc.

ROW 24 (RS) Ch 3, dc in each stitch across—12 dc.

Fasten off. Weave in the ends.

BACK PANEL

Join two sets of two squares together using a slip stitch through only the back loops as described for Front Panel. Next, partially join those two-motif sets along one edge, working a slip stitch through the bottom 5 stitches only—this will leave a slight opening at the top, making the shirt easier to put on and take off. Fasten off. Weave in the ends.

Back Top Edging

ROW 1 (RS) With right side facing, join yarn at the top right corner of the back panel, ch 3, dc in next 26 stitches, (dc, ch 8, sl st) in corner stitch [button loop made], sl st down the left-hand side of the 2nd square and back up the right-hand side of the 3rd square, ch 3, continue to dc in each stitch across the top edge of the remaining 2 squares.

Fasten off. Weave in the ends.

ASSEMBLING BODICE

With right sides facing, line up the edge of the Left Strap with the top left edge of the Back Panel, and join the pieces with a row of slip stitches. Repeat the join for the Right Strap.

NECKLINE TRIM

ROW 1 (RS) With right side facing, join yarn at the corner of the 3rd motif from the right on back (opposite the button loop motif), and slip stitch evenly around the entire inside top edge of the neckline (until you reach the button loop). Fasten off. Weave in the ends.

OUTER EDGING

ROUND 1 (RS) With right side facing, attach yarn on the back right corner of the bodice, ch 1 then sc around the outer edge of the piece, working (2 sc, ch 1) in the stitch before each corner and working 2 sc in the side of each dc row along straps, sl st in first sc to join.
ROUND 2 *Ch 1, hdc in next stitch, ch 1, sl st in next sc; repeat from * around, sl st in first stitch to join. Fasten off. Weave in the ends.

SEWING SHIRT BOTTOM

Sized for S (M, L)

For fabric bottom, cut two rectangles of fabric to 18 (20, 22)" (45.5 [51, 56]cm) deep by 22 (24, 26)" (56 [61, 66]cm) wide. Using a fabric marker, mark one wider edge of each rectangle 4½ (5½, 5½)" (11.5 [14, 14]cm) in from either side with a small dot.

NOTE: *Use a ½" (13mm) seam allowance unless otherwise noted.*

About ¼" (6mm) from the raw edge, baste the top of one rectangle between the two marked dots with long, gathering stitches. It's helpful to use a contrasting thread to sew the basting stitches, since you will pull them out later. Do *not* backstitch at the beginning or end of your basting seam, and leave your thread ends

long at both the beginning and end of the seam. Pull the thread ends to gather up the stitches on the top edge of your fabric until the length between the marked dots measures 10" (25.5cm) wide. Knot both long ends of the basting thread to hold the gathers in place.

Cut a length of bias tape slightly longer than the top edge of the fabric. Unfold the tape and place it so that the thinnest fold with the raw edge lines up with the raw basted edge of the shirt. Pin the tape in place. Sew the tape to the shirt along the first fold of the bias tape. Cut the thread and fold the bias tape around the shirt, encasing the raw gathered edge. Pin the back fold in place on the wrong side of the fabric. On the front side of the shirt, stitch down the folded line of the bias tape, making sure to catch the raw edge and the back fold of the bias tape. Use a seam ripper to rip out any basting stitches that still show.

Repeat the gathering process, and attach bias tape as described above on the 2nd rectangle to make the shirt back.

ASSEMBLING SHIRT

Stack the shirt front and back together with bias-tape edges matched and right sides together. Sew down the two short sides of the rectangle. Clip the edges with pinking shears to finish the seam, or

sew a zigzag just outside of the seam you just sewed. Press the seam. You now have a fabric tube.

Turn the tube right side out. Turn the bottom, ungathered fabric edge under 1" (2.5cm) and press the fold. Turn the 1" (2.5cm) fold under ½" (13mm) and press the fold. Stitch the hem in place along the inside fold.

FINISHING

Pin the bodice front to the front of the shirt, centering the crochet work over the fabric. The trimmed edge of the bodice should just overlap the bias tape edge. Hand-sew the bodice to the top edge of the shirt. Repeat with the back of the bodice and the back of the shirt bottom. Using a sewing needle and thread, attach one button directly across from the button loop on the back panel.

USING A STORE-BOUGHT SHIRT ▫ ▪ ● ▪ ●

Align the bodice with the straps of a loose-fitting tank top (an oversized cotton tank works best). Cut the straps and top of the tank top off just above the bottom of the armholes. Cut a piece of bias tape slightly longer than the circumference of the cut edge and apply it to the edge of the entire shirt as described in *Sewing Shirt Bottom*, then follow the directions in *Finishing*.

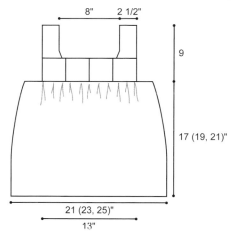

8" 2 1/2"

9

17 (19, 21)"

21 (23, 25)"

13"

Construction Diagram

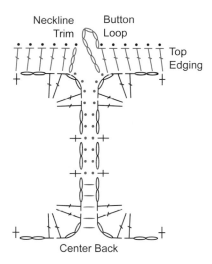

Neckline   Button
Trim   Loop

Top
Edging

Center Back

STITCH KEY

◯ = chain (ch)

• = slip st (sl st)

+ = single crochet (sc)

T = double crochet (dc)

Wavy Waistline Skirt

Accent your waistline with colorful crocheted details. This geometric trim works up quickly and is sure to transform any plain-jane garment in your closet. If you can't decide which skirt to embellish, try making a belt instead—see the variation at the end of the pattern.

Skill Level Intermediate

Finished Measurements

Trim measures 2¾" (7cm) wide; the length of the trim is determined by your garment.

Materials

- 1 skein each of Louet *Gems Worsted Weight*, 100% merino wool, 175 yd (160m), 3½ oz (100g), in #54 Teal (A), #47 Terra Cotta (B), #70 White (C), and #05 Goldilocks (D) 🌕
- Size F-5 (3.75mm) crochet hook, or size to obtain gauge
- Skirt to embellish (choose one with no elastic at the waist)
- Yarn needle
- T-pins, iron, and blocking board
- Straight pins
- Sewing machine or hand-sewing needle
- Sewing threads to match yarns

Gauge

2 shells in Round 1 of pattern measures 3" (7.5cm) in length.

Determining Trim Length

For the best results, choose a skirt that has a zipper rather than one that stretches to fit your waist. Measure the waistline and subtract about 2" (5cm) (for the zipper space and the extra width of the trim created by Rounds 2–4). Refer to *Determining Foundation Chain Length* (page 33) for instructions on how to determine the number of chains in the foundation chain for your length of trim.

Special Stitch

SPIKE STITCH Insert hook in next corresponding sc 2 rows below, yo, draw yarn through stitch and up to level of work, yo, draw yarn through 2 lps on hook.

MAKING TRIM

With yarn A, ch a multiple of 6 plus 2 stitches.

ROUND 1 (RS) Sc in 2nd ch from hook, *sk next 2 ch, 7 tr in next stitch (shell made), sk next 2 ch, sc in next ch*; repeat from * to * across, ending with (sc, ch 2, sc) in last ch. Working across opposite side of foundation ch, repeat from * to * around, ch 1, sl st in first sc to join. Fasten off.

ROUND 2 With right side facing, working in BL of stitches, join yarn B in first sc, ch 5 (counts as dc, ch 2), dc in same sc, *hdc in next tr, sc in next tr, sl st in each of next 3 tr, sc in next tr, hdc in next tr, dc in next sc*; repeat from *to * across to next corner, ending with (dc, ch 2, dc) in last sc to form corner, working across short end of trim, work 4 sc evenly spaced across end, (dc, ch 2, dc) in next sc to form corner**; repeat from * to ** across bottom and second short end, sl st in 3rd ch of beginning ch to join. Fasten off B.

ROUND 3 With right side facing, join yarn C in first ch-2 sp, ch 1, (sc, ch 2, sc) in first ch-2 sp, working in BL of stitches, sc in each of next 8 stitches, *spike stitch (insert hook into top of sc from row 1), sc in next 7 stitches*, repeat from * to * across to next corner, sc in next dc, (sc, ch 2, sc) in next ch-2 sp, then sc in next 6 stitches on short end of trim**, (sc, ch 1, sc) in next ch-2 sp, sc in next 8 stitches; repeat from * to ** once, sl st in first sc to join. Fasten off C.

ROUND 4 With right side facing, working in BL of stitches, join yarn D in first sc to the left of first ch-2 sp, ** *hdc in next sc, dc in next sc, hdc in next sc, sl st in next 2 sc; repeat from * across, ending long edge with sl st in sc before ch-2 sp, sl st in next 2 ch, repeat from * twice, sl st in first sc on opposite long edge, repeat from ** around, sl st in first sl st to join.

Fasten off. Weave in the ends.

FINISHING

Block the trim and let it dry.

Carefully pin the trim in place along the waistline of your skirt. Line up the short edges of the trim with the edges of the zipper or button closure. Sew the trim to the waistline with coordinating thread. Machine or hand-sew a line of stitches across the top, bottom, and center of the trim, changing the thread to match the color of yarn you are sewing across.

MAKE A BELT ● ● ● ● ●

If you're not ready to commit, try making this trim into a belt instead. Here's how: Measure your waist and add 8" (20.5cm), then make the trim to match those measurements. Cut a piece of 2" (5cm) grosgrain ribbon 8" (20.5cm) shorter than your belt and stitch the back side of the trim to the ribbon for stability, leaving 8" (20.5cm) on one side raw. Stitch the ribbon-backed short end around a belt buckle, and you'll be all set! The buckle prong will easily slide through a space in the stitchwork on the unbacked end of your belt.

STITCH KEY

- ⌒ = chain (ch)
- • = slip st (sl st)
- + = single crochet (sc)
- ⊤ = half double crochet (hdc)
- ⊤ = double crochet (dc)
- ⊤ = treble crochet (tr)
- + = spike st
- } = worked in back loop only

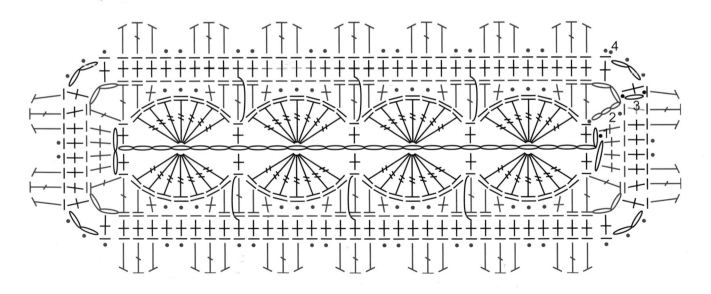

Pretty Petals Tank

Soft, affordable yarn makes it easy to transform a basic racer-back tank top into a stunning new look. The lightweight open medallions look and feel great against summer skin or layered over another bold tank. You can also make this collar for a halter top (see the variation at the end of the instructions), or try these motifs around the collar of a scoop-neck top.

Skill Level Intermediate

Finished Measurements

Completed collar measures 30"
(75cm) long and approximately 3¼"
(8.5cm) wide.

For a longer collar, make more Small
Petal Medallions and Circle Motifs.

Materials

- 1 skein Coats and Clark *Red Heart Lustersheen*, 100% acrylic, 335 yds (306m), 4 oz (113g), #913 Warm Red (2)
- Size F-5 (3.75mm) crochet hook, or size to obtain gauge
- Racer-back tank or scoop-neck tank to embellish
- T-pins, iron, and blocking board
- Hand-sewing needle and matching sewing thread
- Yarn needle
- 4 to 6 sew-on snaps, size 2/0
- 2 hook-and-eye closures (optional, for variation)

Gauge

Completed Small Medallion
measures 3½" (9cm) in diameter
across widest point.

Special Stitches

DOUBLE CROCHET 3 TOGETHER
CLUSTER (dc3tog) (Yo, insert hook
in stitch, yo, draw yarn through
stitch, yo, draw yarn through 2 lps
on hook) 3 times in same stitch, yo,
draw yarn through 4 lps on hook.

DOUBLE CROCHET 4 TOGETHER
CLUSTER (dc4tog) (Yo, insert hook
in stitch, yo, draw yarn through
stitch, yo, draw yarn through 2 lps
on hook) 4 times in same stitch, yo,
draw yarn through 5 lps on hook.

SMALL MEDALLION (MAKE 8)

Ch 8, join with a sl st to form a ring.

ROUND 1 (RS) Ch 3, dc3tog in ring
(counts as dc4tog), (ch 6, dc4tog)
7 times in ring, ch 6, sl st in first
cluster to join—8 clusters, 8 ch-6 lps.

ROUND 2 *Ch 1, (hdc, 3 dc, ch 3, sc
in 3rd ch from hook for picot, 3 dc,
hdc) in next ch-6 lp, ch 1, sl st in
next cluster; repeat from * around,
ending with sl st in first sl st to
join—8 petals.

Fasten off, leaving a 10" (25.5cm)
tail for joining motifs. Weave in the
center end.

LARGE MEDALLION (MAKE 1)

Ch 8, join with a sl st to form a ring.

ROUND 1 (RS) Ch 3, dc3tog in ring
(counts as dc4tog), (ch 6, dc4tog) 7
times in ring, ch 3, dc in first cluster
to join (counts as last ch-6 lp)—8
clusters, 8 ch-6 lps.

ROUND 2 Ch 1, sc in first lp, ch 6,
*(sc, ch 4, sc) in next ch-6 loop, ch 6;
repeat from * around, ending with sc
in first lp, ch 2, hdc in first sc to join
(counts as last ch-4 lp)—8 ch-4 lps; 8
ch-6 lps.

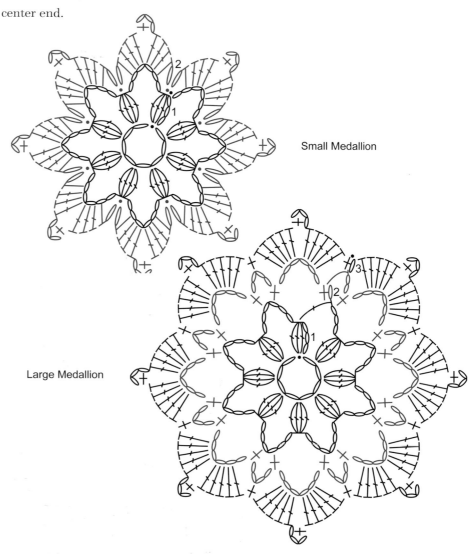

Small Medallion

Large Medallion

ROUND 3 Ch 1, sc in first lp, *(5 dc, ch 3, sc in 3rd ch from hook for picot, 5 dc) in next ch-6 lp, sc in next ch-4 lp; repeat from * around, omitting last sc, sl st in first sc to join—8 petals.

Fasten off, leaving a 10" (25.5cm) tail for joining motifs. Weave in the center end.

STITCH KEY
- ◯ = chain (ch)
- • = slip st (sl st)
- ✝ = single crochet (sc)
- ⊤ = half double crochet (hdc)
- ⊤ = double crochet (dc)
- = dc4tog
- = dc3tog
- = picot

CONNECTOR CIRCLES

Circle Motif A (Make 8)

Ch 6, join with a sl st to form a ring.
ROUND 1 (RS) Ch 2 (counts as hdc),
14 hdc in ring—15 hdc.

Fasten off, leaving a 10" (25.5cm)
tail for joining motifs. Weave in the
center end.

Circle Motif A

Circle Motif B (Make 8)

Ch 6, join with a sl st to form a ring.
ROUND 1 (RS) Ch 2 (counts as hdc),
19 hdc in ring—20 hdc.

Fasten off, leaving a 10" (25.5cm)
tail for joining motifs. Weave in the
center end.

Circle Motif B

FINISHING

Using yarn tails or a length of
yarn, sew four Connector Circles
and two Small Medallions to the
center Large Medallion as shown
in the construction diagram. Center
the medallion panel over the shirt
collar, making sure the bottom edge
overlaps the shirt collar by at least
1" (2.5cm) all the way across the
collar. Pin the panel in place and sew

only the bottom edge of the panel
to the shirt, following the outermost
edges of the petals and circles. Be
careful not to sew the centers of the
medallions, or you won't be able to
cut away the shirt.

After sewing the panel in place, cut
the straps from the front of the shirt
(leave them connected in the back
for reference). Carefully cut the tank
about ½" (13mm) above the line of
stitches you just made, following the
curves of the seam. Discard the cut
fabric. Fold the cut shirt edge away
from the medallion panel, rolling
the raw edge under if possible,
and whip stitch the edge in place,
making sure that none of the shirt
shows through the open petal design.

Attach the rest of the collar to the
medallion panel as shown in the
diagram. Use a yarn needle and
lengths of yarn to piece the collar,
and refer to the existing shirt straps
for placement. Try on the shirt.
Adjust the collar around your neck,
then pin the straps to the back panel
of the tank as desired. If you are
able to take the shirt off comfortably
with the flowers pinned, stitch
flower ends directly to the back
panel of the tank. If the collar is too
narrow to fit over your head, stitch
two or three snap studs to the petals
on each end, and two or three snap
sockets to each side of the back panel
of the tank—fasten the collar after
the shirt is on.

Cut off any remaining tank straps
and sew the raw edges to the inside
of the shirt to conceal them.

CHART KEY
S = Small Medallion
L = Large Medallion
A = Circle Motif A
B = Circle Motif B

Construction Diagram

MAKE IT A HALTER TOP

You can also sew this collar to
a halter top. Follow the same
instructions, but instead of sewing
the flowers to the back tank panel,
stitch them to each other to close
the collar. Or, sew two hooks on
the right side flower end and two
eye closures on the left side flower
end. Fasten each hook and eye to
close the collar.

Like-New Shoes

Give your tired shoes a mini-makeover with these easy trims. They work up so quickly that you'll be able to coordinate a pair with every outfit. You'll only need a tiny bit of yarn for each shoe, so try working with odds and ends you have on hand.

Skill Level Beginner

Finished Measurements

The completed Chain Stitch Trim measures ⅛" (3mm) wide; the length of the trim is determined by your shoe. One completed Ruffle Trim measures ¾" (2cm) wide by 3¼" (8.5cm) long.

Materials

* 1 ball Southwest Trading Company *Vickie Howell Craft*, 65% organic cotton, 35% milk fiber 137 yd (125 m), 1¾ oz (50 g), #769 Jennifer (A) and #779 Share (B) **2**
* Size D-3 (3.25mm) crochet hook (for ruffle trim) or size F-5 (3.75mm) crochet hook (for chain trim), or size to obtain gauge.
* Yarn needle
* Shoes to embellish (look for a pair that's easy to sew through)
* Hand-sewing needle
* Sewing thread to match yarn
* Fabric glue (optional)

Gauge

Gauge is not critical for this project. Refer to the finished measurements, and make one ruffle or one length of chain to check gauge.

RUFFLE TRIM (MAKE 2)

With yarn A and a size D-3 (3.25 mm) hook, ch 14.
ROW 1 (WS) Sc in 2nd ch from hook, sc in each ch across, turn—13 sc.

ROW 2 Ch 2 (counts as first hdc), (3 dc, hdc) in first sc, *hdc in next sc, (hdc, 3 dc, hdc) in next sc; repeat from * across.

Fasten off. Weave in the ends.

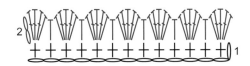

STITCH KEY

◠ = chain (ch)

+ = single crochet (sc)

T = half double crochet (hdc)

⊤ = double crochet (dc)

NOTE: *If you'd like a longer ruffle, work a longer foundation chain. Make sure to work a multiple of 2 chain stitches.*

ATTACHING RUFFLES

Sew one ruffle to the toe of each shoe as shown in the photograph at right. Use a sharp needle to sew the foundation chain loops to the front edge of the shoe opening, then tack some of the ruffles in place from the inside of the shoe. Knot off the thread and secure the end with a dab of fabric glue, if desired.

CHAIN STITCH TRIM

Make two foundation chains, each about 1" (2.5cm) longer than the opening of your shoe. Fasten off the yarn and weave in the ends.

Place one end of the chain trim at the instep of the shoe and sew the trim around the entire edge. When you reach the beginning of the trim again, overlap the excess 1" (2.5cm) and securely sew the trim in place. You can also try gluing the trim in place, but be sure to test the glue first to make sure it won't discolor the shoe or yarn.

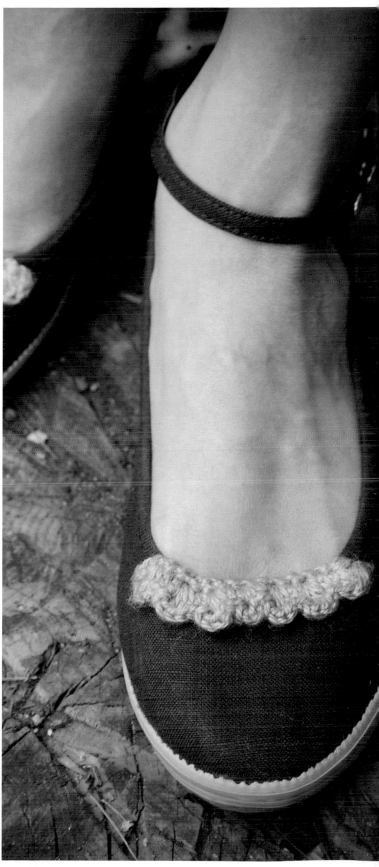

Tree Tote

Combine simple geometric shapes with lacy motifs to make this cute tree tote. Vary the color, weight, and texture of the yarn you choose and you'll create your own magical forest. These appliqués would also look cute on the hem of a skirt!

Skill Level Easy

Finished measurements

The Small Flower Tree Top measures 2⅝" (6.5cm) in diameter; the Trunk measures 3½" (9cm) long and ⅝" (1.5cm) wide. The Large Flower Tree Top measures 4¼" (11cm) in diameter; the Trunk measures 5¼" (13.5cm) long and ⅝" (1.5cm) wide.

Materials

- 1 skein each Brown Sheep *Cotton Fleece*, 80% cotton, 20% merino wool, 215 yd (197m), 3½ oz (100g), #380 Dusty Sage (A), #365 Peridot (B), #455 Willow Leaf (C), #460 Jungle Green (D), and #825 Truffle (E) ③
- Size F-5 (3.75mm) crochet hook, or size to obtain gauge.
- Tote bag to embellish (at least 14" [35.5cm] x 14½" [37cm], excluding handle)
- Hand-sewing needle
- Sewing threads to match yarns

Gauge

Although gauge is not critical for this project, you can refer to finished measurements for tree parts. Each piece works up as quickly as a gauge swatch.

Special Stitch

PICOT Ch 3, sc in 3rd ch from hook.

LARGE FLOWER TREE

Tree Top

With yarn D, make a magic ring.

ROUND 1 (RS) Ch 3 (counts as dc here and throughout), 9 dc in ring, sl st in beginning ch to join—10 dc.

ROUND 2 Ch 3, dc in first dc, 2 dc in each remaining dc of round, sl st in beginning ch to join—20 dc.

ROUND 3 Ch 3, *2 dc in next dc, dc in next dc; repeat from * around, ending with 2 dc in last dc, sl st in beginning ch to join—30 dc.

ROUND 4 Ch 3, dc in next dc, *2 dc in next dc, dc in each of next 2 dc; repeat from * around, ending with 2 dc in last dc, sl st in beginning ch to join—40 dc.

ROUND 5 Ch 3, dc in each of next 2 dc, *2 dc in next dc, dc in each of next 3 dc; repeat from * around, ending with 2 dc in last dc, sl st in beginning ch to join—50 dc.

Fasten off and weave in the ends.

Tree Trunk

With yarn E, ch 30.

ROW 1 (RS) Dc in 4th ch from hook, dc in each ch across—28 dc.

Fasten off and leave a long tail for sewing. Sew the tree trunk to the tree top.

Large Flower

With yarn B, make a magic ring.

ROUND 1 (RS) Ch 1, 8 sc in ring, sl st in first sc to join—8 sc.

ROUND 2 Ch 1, sc in first sc, ch 4, (sc, ch 4) in each sc around, ending with ch 2, hdc in first sc instead of

last ch-4 lp (this will put yarn in the correct position for the next round)—8 ch-4 lps.

ROUND 3 Ch 1, sc in first lp, ch 4, (sc, ch 4) in each ch-4 lp around, sl st in first sc to join—8 ch-4 lps.

ROUND 4 *(Sc, hdc, 3 dc, hdc, sc) in next ch-4 lp (shell made), sl st in next sc; repeat from * around, sl st in first sl st to join—8 shells.

Fasten off. Weave in the ends.

POINTED FLOWER TREE

Tree Top

With yarn C, work same as Large Flower Tree Top through Round 4.

Fasten off. Weave in the ends.

Tree Trunk

With yarn E, ch 28.

ROW 1 (RS) Dc in 4th ch from hook, dc in each ch across—26 dc.

Fasten off and leave a long tail for sewing. Sew the tree trunk to the tree top.

Pointed Flower

With yarn D, ch 8 and join with a sl st to form a ring.

ROUND 1 (RS) Ch 1, 12 sc in ring, sl st in first sc to join—12 sc.

ROUND 2 Ch 1, (dc, tr) in first sc, picot, (tr, dc, ch 1, sl st) in next sc, *(sl st, ch 1, dc, tr) in next sc, picot, (tr, dc, ch 1, sl st) in next sc; repeat from * around, sl st in first stitch to join—6 picots.

Fasten off and leave a long tail

for sewing. Sew the flower to the center of the tree top. Weave in the remaining ends.

SMALL FLOWER TREE

Tree Top

With yarn A, work same as Large Flower Tree Top through Round 3.

Fasten off. Weave in the ends.

Tree Trunk

With yarn E, ch 19.

ROW 1 (RS) Dc in 4th ch from hook, dc in each ch across—17 dc.

Fasten off and leave a long tail for sewing. Sew the tree trunk to the tree top.

Small Flower

With yarn C, make a magic ring.

ROUND 1 (RS) Ch 1, 8 sc in ring, sl st in first sc to join—8 sc.

ROUND 2 Ch 1, sc in first sc, ch 4, (sc, ch 4) in each sc around, sl st in first sc to join—8 ch-4 lps.

Fasten off and leave a long tail for sewing. Sew the small flower to the center of the tree top. Weave in the remaining ends.

RINGED WREATH TREE

Tree Top

With yarn B, work same as Large Flower Tree Top through Round 3.

ROUND 4 Ch 2 (counts as hdc), hdc in next dc, *2 hdc in next dc, hdc in each of next 2 dc; repeat from * around, ending with hdc in each

of last 2 dc, sl st in beginning ch to join—40 hdc.

Fasten off. Weave in the ends.

Tree Trunk

With yarn E, ch 21.

ROW 1 (RS) Dc in 4th ch from hook and each ch across—19 dc.

Fasten off, leaving a long tail for sewing. Sew the tree trunk to the tree top.

Ringed Wreath

NOTE: *Wreath is worked in a straight line. Sew the crocheted line together at the short ends to form a circle.*

ROUND 1 (RS) With yarn A, *ch 3, 4 sc in 2nd ch from hook; repeat from * 6 times, ch 3, 8 sc in 2nd ch from hook. Working across opposite side, sl st in 8th sc from hook, **sl st in next sc, 4 sc in 2nd ch of next ch-3, sk 2 sc from opposite side and sl st in next sc, repeat from ** across row, ending with sc in first ch of round.

Fasten off, leaving a long tail for sewing, and sew ends of trim together to form a circle. Sew the wreath to the center of the tree top. Weave in the remaining ends.

FINISHING

Place the assembled trees on the tote as shown in the photograph, or as desired. Pin tree tops in place. With thread to match each tree and trunk you are attaching, hand-sew the tree top, and then the trunk, in place. Work from the inside of the bag and make stitches small so they are well concealed by the yarn, being careful not to accidentally stitch through both sides of the bag.

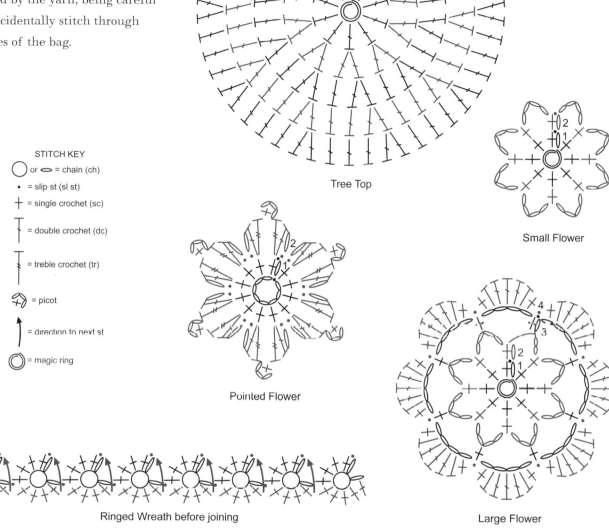

Tree Top

Small Flower

Pointed Flower

Large Flower

STITCH KEY

◯ or ⬭ = chain (ch)

• = slip st (sl st)

+ = single crochet (sc)

⊤ = double crochet (dc)

⊤ = treble crochet (tr)

= picot

↑ = direction to next st

◎ = magic ring

Ringed Wreath before joining

Lacy Headband

Add a touch of luxury to this easy-to-make headband by working it in a super-soft silk blend yarn—it takes less than a skein. Attach small lengths of elastic with a bit of sewing, and your new hair accessory will be both stylish and snug. For extra flair, try accenting this piece with your favorite flower motif from the Stitch Dictionary, beginning on page III.

Skill Level Beginner

Finished Measurements

Completed headband measures 18" (45.5cm) in circumference (including elastic) and 4" (10cm) wide.

Materials

- 1 ball of Cascade Yarns *Venezia Worsted*, 70% merino wool, 30% silk, 218 yd (200m), 3½ oz (100g), #120 black (3)
- Size F-5 (3.75mm) crochet hook, or size to obtain gauge
- 6" (15cm) length of ⅜"- (1cm) wide black elastic
- Yarn needle
- T-pins, iron, and blocking board
- Sewing needle and matching sewing thread

Gauge

To work a gauge swatch, ch 26 and follow pattern for all 7 rows. Once blocked, the swatch should measure 4" (10cm) across and 3" (7.5cm) wide.

HEADBAND

Ch 86.

ROW 1 (RS) (Sc, ch 3, sc) in 8th ch from hook, *ch 5, sk next 4 ch, (sc, ch 3, sc) in next ch; repeat from * across to last 3 ch, ending with ch 2, sk next 2 ch, dc in last ch, turn—15 ch-5 lps.

ROW 2 Ch 1, sc in first dc, *ch 5, (sc, ch 3, sc) in center ch of next ch-5 lp; repeat from * across, ch 5, sc in 5th ch of turning ch, turn—16 ch-5 lps.

ROW 3 Ch 5 (counts as dc, ch 2 here and throughout), (sc, ch 3, sc) in center ch of next ch-5 lp, *ch 5, (sc, ch 3, sc) in center ch of next ch-5 lp; repeat from * across to last ch-5 lp, ch 2, dc in last sc, turn—15 ch-5 lps.

ROWS 4–6 Repeat Rows 2 and 3 once, then repeat Row 2 once.

ROW 7 *Ch 5, sc in center ch of next ch-5 lp, *ch 4, sc in center ch of next ch-5 lp; repeat from * across to last ch-5 lp, ch 2, dc in last sc.

Fasten off. Weave in the ends. The top edge of the work is the back edge of the headband.

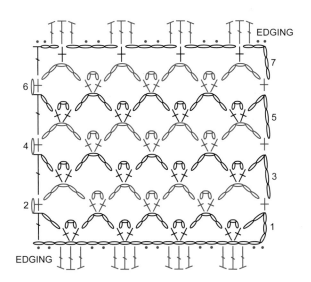

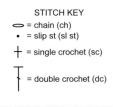

STITCH KEY

⌒ = chain (ch)

• = slip st (sl st)

+ = single crochet (sc)

T = double crochet (dc)

Edging

With right side facing, join yarn in the right-hand corner of one long edge, sl st in next stitch, *dc in each of next 3 stitches, sl st in next 2 stitches; repeat from * across

Repeat the edging across the opposite long edge of the headband.

FINISHING

Block the headband and let it dry.

Cut the elastic into two 3" (7.5cm) lengths. Referring to placement diagram, overlap ¾" (2cm) of the elastic underneath the headband at the top right corner and sew it in place. Overlap ¾" (2cm) of the opposite end of the elastic underneath the opposite top corner of the headband and sew it in place. Sew the second length of elastic to the bottom corners in the same manner.

Construction Diagram

Dainty Earrings

Pretty earrings crafted from delicate crochet thread work up quickly and make great gifts. If you're into beading, try combining these pieces with beads and chain for an eclectic look.

Skill Level Easy

Finished Measurements

Hoop Earrings measure 1⅛" (3cm) across; Doily Earrings measure ¼" (3cm) across; Leaf Earrings measure 1½" (4cm) long.

Materials

- 1 ball Coats and Clark *Aunt Lydia's Classic Crochet Thread*, Size 10, 100% mercerized cotton, 350 yd (320m) in #226 Natural (A) and #397 Wasabi (B) 🔟
- Size 7 (1.5mm) steel crochet hook, or size to obtain gauge
- Yarn needle
- 1 pair ear wires (per set)
- Flat-nose pliers

Gauge

Although gauge is not critical for this project, you can refer to finished measurements for final earring sizes. Each earring works up as quickly as a gauge swatch.

LEAF EARRINGS (MAKE 2)

With yarn A, ch 8.

ROUND 1 (RS) Sc in 2nd ch from hook, hdc in next 2 ch, dc in next 3 ch, 8 dc in last chain, working across opposite side of foundation ch, dc in each of next 3 ch, hdc in each of next 2 ch, sc in next ch, sl st to first sc to join—20 stitches.

ROUND 2 Ch 1, sc in first stitch, sc in each of next 6 stitches, 2 sc in each of next 6 stitches, sc in each remaining stitch of round, ch 1, sl st to first sc to join, turn—26 sc.

ROUND 3 With wrong side facing, ch 2 (counts as hdc), sl st in first stitch, (hdc, sl st) in each stitch around, sl st in first sl st to join—27 hdc.

Fasten off. Weave in the ends.

HOOP EARRINGS (MAKE 2)

With yarn B, ch 12, join with a sl st to form a ring.

ROUND 1 (RS) Ch 1, work (3 sc, 3 hdc, 6 dc, 3 hdc, 3 sc) into ring, sl st in first sc to join—18 stitches.

ROUND 2 With RS facing, join yarn A in first sc, ch 1, sc in each of first 3 sc, 2 hdc in each of next 3 hdc, 2 dc in each of next 6 dc, 2 hdc in each of next 2 hdc, sc in each of next 3 sc, sl st in first sc to join—30 stitches.

ROUND 3 With yarn B, sl st in each stitch around, sl st in first sc to join—30 stitches.

Fasten off. Weave in the ends.

DOILY EARRINGS (MAKE 2)

With yarn A, make a magic ring.

ROUND 1 (RS) Ch 3 (counts as hdc, ch 1), (hdc, ch 1) 9 times in ring, sl st in 2nd ch of beginning ch to join—10 ch-1 sps.

ROUND 2 Ch 5 (counts as sc, ch 4), (sc, ch 4) in each hdc around, sl st in first ch to join—10 ch-4 lps.

ROUND 3 Sl st in each of next 2 chs, ch 5 (counts as sc, ch 4), (sc, ch 4) in each ch-4 lp around, sl st in first ch to join—10 ch-4 lps.

Fasten off. Weave in the ends.

FINISHING (ALL EARRINGS)

With flat-nosed pliers, grasp one half of the earring loop and turn it out about 45 degrees. Slip the loop under the V of the stitch in the top center of each earring. For the Doily Earrings, slip the loop through any ch-4 space. Close the loop with the pliers and repeat for the other earring.

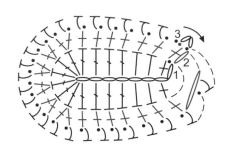

Leaf Earrings

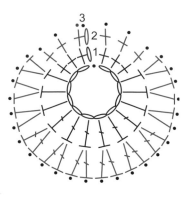

Hoop Earrings

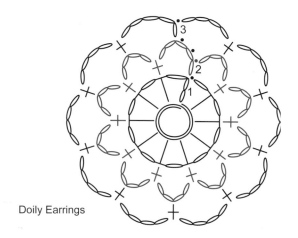

Doily Earrings

STITCH KEY

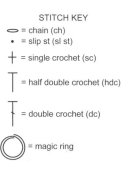

⬯ = chain (ch)

• = slip st (sl st)

+ = single crochet (sc)

T = half double crochet (hdc)

T̄ = double crochet (dc)

◯ = magic ring

Bird Brooches

Add a simple avian silhouette to your attire for a fresh, springy look. These birds work up quickly, and with a bit of fabric stiffener they're sturdy enough to pin to your coat. You can also use the unstarched silhouette as an adornment on a tote or tee, or even to patch up a tear in your favorite jeans.

Finished Measurements

4" (10cm) long from beak to tail.

Materials

- 1 ball of Filatura Di Crosa *Millefili Fine*, 100% cotton, 136 yd (125m), 1¾ oz (50g), #254 forest green (A), #155 sky blue (B), and #208 lilac (C) ⟨2⟩
- Size B-1 (2.25mm) crochet hook, or size to obtain gauge
- Yarn needle
- Commercial fabric stiffener or sugar water solution (see Lace Bowl, page 108, for details)
- 2" (5cm) pin back
- E6000 glue

Gauge

Gauge is not critical for this project; one completed bird measures 4" (10cm) long from beak to tail.

BIRD SILHOUETTE

Body

Make a magic ring.

ROW 1 (RS) Ch 3 (counts as dc throughout), 5 dc in ring, turn—6 dc.

ROW 2 Ch 3, dc in first stitch, 2 dc in each stitch across, ending with 2 dc in top of turning ch, turn—12 dc.

ROUND 3 Ch 3, dc in first stitch, *dc in next stitch, 2 dc in next stitch; repeat from * across, ending with dc in top of turning ch, ch 8 (for tail), working in bottom loops of ch stitches (sl st in 2nd ch from hook, sc in next ch, hdc in next 2 ch, dc in next 3 ch), working across straight

edge of body, 2 dc in each of next 3 row-end dc, dc in magic ring, 2 dc in each of next 2 row-end dc, (dc, 8 tr, ch 3, sl st in 3rd ch from hook for picot, tr, dc, hdc, sc) in base of beginning ch of Round 3 for head, sl st in top of beginning ch.

Fasten off. Weave in the ends.

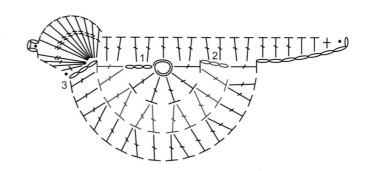

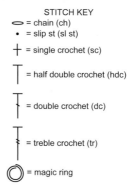

STITCH KEY

⊂⊃ = chain (ch)

• = slip st (sl st)

+ = single crochet (sc)

T = half double crochet (hdc)

┴ = double crochet (dc)

‡ = treble crochet (tr)

◯ = magic ring

FINISHING

To stiffen the birds, mix 50 percent commercial fabric stiffener with 50 percent water and stiffen following the manufacturer's instructions. If you prefer a home-made sugar and water solution, refer to the finishing instructions for the Lace Bowl on page 108. Allow the birds to dry completely. Attach a pin back to the back side of each brooch using E6000 glue or another strong jewelry adhesive.

Mod Cross Pillow

This modern pillow is a perfect way to experiment with color and add some pop flair to your living room. Designed by Tricia Royal, the pattern is super simple to execute, even for beginners. Each side of the pillow features granny square motifs in a different color combination, so you can change it to suit your mood. If you're running short on time, crochet only the squares and sew them to a store-bought pillow.

Skill Level Beginner

Finished Measurements

Finished pillow measures 16" (40.5cm) by 16" (40.5cm), one granny square motif measures 4¾" (12cm) by 4¾" (12cm).

Materials

- Blue Sky Alpacas *Dyed Cotton,* 100% cotton, 150 yd (137m), 3½ oz (100g); 4 skeins of #601 Poppy (MC), 1 skein of #630 Caribbean (A), and 1 skein of #604 Aloe (B) ③
- Size F-5 (3.75mm) and G-6 (4mm) crochet hooks, or sizes to obtain gauge
- 16" (40.5) x 16" (40.5) pillow form
- Scissors
- Yarn needle
- Ruler or tape measure
- Straight pins

Gauge

With F-5 (3.75mm) hook, 15 sc worked over 15 rows measures 4½" (11.5cm) by 4" (10cm). With G-6 (4mm) hook, first 2 rounds of motif measure 3½" (9cm) by 3½" (9cm).

PILLOW CASE PANELS (MAKE 2, 1 EACH FOR FRONT AND BACK)

With MC yarn and size F-5 (3.75 mm) hook, ch 55.

ROW 1 (RS) Sc in 2nd ch from hook, sc in each ch across, turn—54 sc.

ROW 2 Ch 1, sc in each sc across, turn—54 sc.

Repeat Row 2 until piece measures 16" (40.5) in length.

Fasten off. Weave in the ends.

GRANNY SQUARE MOTIFS (MAKE 5 IN THE FOLLOWING COLOR COMBINATIONS: A/B AND B/A)

With yarn A and size G-6 (4mm) crochet hook, ch 5, join with a sl st to form a ring.

ROUND 1 (RS) With yarn A, ch 3 (counts as first dc here and throughout), 2 dc into ring, ch 2 (corner made), *3 dc in ring, ch 2; repeat from * twice more, sl st in top of beginning ch to join—4 ch-2 corner sps; 12 dc. Fasten off.

ROUND 2 With right side facing, join yarn B in any corner ch-2 space, ch 3, (2 dc, ch 2, 3 dc) in first space, *ch 1, (3 dc, ch 2, 3 dc) in next corner; repeat from * twice more, ch 1, sl st in top of beginning ch to join—4 ch-2 corner sps; 4 ch-1 sps; 24 dc. Fasten off.

ROUND 3 Continuing with yarn B, sl st to next ch-2 corner space, ch 3, (2 dc, ch 2, 3 dc) in first space, ch 1, 3 dc in next ch-1 space, ch 1, *(3 dc, ch 2, 3 dc) in next corner ch-2 space, ch 1, 3 dc in next ch-1 space, ch 1; repeat from * twice more, sl st in top of beginning ch to join—4 ch-2 corner sps; 8 ch-1 sps; 36 dc.

Fasten off. Weave in the ends.

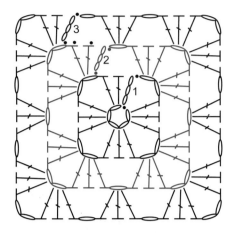

Granny Square Motif

FINISHING

Block the granny squares to 4¾" (12cm) by 4¾" (12cm). Block the pillow case panels to 16" (40.5cm) by 16" (40.5cm) .

With the wrong side of the granny square facing the right side of one pillow piece, pin the 5 granny squares with yarn A centers in place according to the measurements given in the construction diagram.

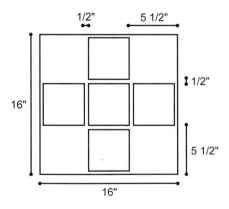

Construction Diagaram

Repeat with the other side of the pillow and the 5 squares with yarn B centers. Sew the squares in place using a yarn needle and lengths of yarn, concealing the stitches in the outside edge of the square motif. Conceal the ends by weaving them in on the wrong side of the pillow.

Edging

ROUND 1 (JOINING ROUND) With the wrong sides of the pillow front and back facing, using a size G-6 (4mm) hook, working through both pillow sides, join MC to the pillow in the stitch just before the top left-hand corner of the pillow. Ch 1, 3 sc in the first corner stitch, sc in each stitch across top edge, *3 sc in next corner, working across side edge, sc in each row-end stitch across*, 3 sc in corner stitch, working across bottom edge, sc in each stitch across, insert pillow form; repeat from * to * across remaining side edge, encasing the pillow form, sl st in first sc to join. Fasten off. Weave in the ends.

Vintage Kitchen Trivets

These cute trivets, designed by Diane Gilleland, are a great project for beginning crocheters. You can use these motifs or choose any lacy circle or square pattern to decorate your own pair. The double layers of yarn will protect your table and countertop from warm pots and pans, and they're sure to add extra charm to your kitchen.

Skill Level Easy

Finished Measurements

Square Trivet measures 7½" (19cm) by 7½" (19cm). Round Trivet measures 7½" (19cm) in diameter.

Materials

- Cascade Yarns *Sierra*, 80% pima cotton, 20% merino wool, 191 yd (175m), 3½ oz (100g) ③
- For Square Trivet: 1 skein each of #13 green (A) and #03 white (B)
- For Round Trivet: 1 skein each of #06 coral (C) and #38 yellow (D)
- Size G-6 (4mm) crochet hook, or size to obtain gauge
- Stitch markers
- Yarn needle
- Hand-sewing needle
- Sewing thread to match backing

Gauge

16 sc worked over 20 rows = 4" (10cm); first 2 rounds of Square Front Motif = 3" (7.5cm) in diameter; first 2 rounds of Round Front Motif = 2½" (6.5cm) in diameter.

Special Stitches

DOUBLE CROCHET 2 TOGETHER CLUSTER (dc2tog) (Yo, insert hook in stitch, yo, draw yarn through stitch, yo, draw yarn through 2 lps on hook) twice in same stitch, yo, draw yarn through 3 lps on hook.

DOUBLE CROCHET 3 TOGETHER CLUSTER (dc3tog) (Yo, insert hook in stitch, yo, draw yarn through stitch, yo, draw yarn through 2 lps on hook) 3 times in same stitch, yo, draw yarn through 4 lps on hook.

DOUBLE CROCHET 4 TOGETHER CLUSTER (dc4tog) (Yo, insert hook in stitch, yo, draw yarn through stitch, yo, draw yarn through 2 lps on hook) 4 times in same stitch, yo, draw yarn through 5 lps on hook.

PICOT Ch 3, sc in 3rd ch from hook.

SQUARE TRIVET

Square Front Motif

With yarn A, ch 6, join with a sl st to form a ring.

ROUND 1 (RS) Ch 3 (counts as dc), 19 dc in ring, sl st to beginning ch to join—20 dc.

ROUND 2 Ch 3, dc3tog in the same stitch (counts as dc4tog here and throughout), (ch 1, dc4tog) in each of next 3 dc, ch 3, *dc4tog in next dc, (ch 1, dc4tog) in each of next 3 dc, ch 3; repeat from * twice, sl st in first dc4tog cluster to join—16 dc4tog; 4 ch-3 corner lps.

ROUND 3 Sl st in next ch-1 sp, ch 3, dc3tog in first ch-1 sp, (ch 1, dc4tog) in each of next 2 ch-1 sps, *ch 2, (dc, ch 1) 3 times in next ch-3 lp, dc in same ch-3 lp, ch 2**, (dc4tog, ch 1) in each of next 2 ch-1 sps, dc4tog in next ch-1 sp; repeat from * around, ending last repeat at **, sl st in first cluster to join—12 dc4tog.

ROUND 4 Sl st in next ch-1 sp, ch 3, dc3tog in first ch-1 sp, ch 1, dc4tog in next ch 1 sp, *ch 2, sk next ch-2 sp, dc in next dc, ch 1, sk next ch-1 sp, dc in next dc, ch 3, sk next ch-1 sp, dc in next dc, ch 1, sk next ch-1 sp, dc in next dc, ch 2**, dc4tog in next ch-1 sp, ch 1, dc4tog in next ch-1 sp; repeat from * around, ending last repeat at **, sl st in first cluster to join—6 dc4tog.

ROUND 5 Sl st in next ch-1 sp, ch 3, dc3tog in first ch-1 sp, *ch 3, sk next cluster and next ch-2 sp, dc in next dc, ch 1, sk next ch-1 sp, dc in next dc, ch 1, 5 dc in next ch-3 sp, ch 1, dc in next dc, ch 1, sk next ch-1 sp, dc in next dc, ch 3, sk next ch-2 sp**, dc4tog in next ch-1 sp; repeat from * around, ending last repeat at **, sl st in first cluster to join—4 dc4tog.

ROUND 6 Ch 3 (counts as dc), *3 dc in next ch-3 lp, (dc in next dc, dc in next ch-1 sp) twice, dc in each of next 2 dc, (dc, tr, dc) in next corner dc, dc in each of next 2 dc, (dc in next ch-1 sp, dc in next dc) twice, 3 dc in next ch-3 lp**, dc in next cluster*; repeat from * to * around, ending last repeat at **, sl st in 3rd ch of beginning ch to join—84 dc; 4 tr.

ROUND 7 Ch 1, sc in first 11 stitches, *3 sc in next corner tr, sc in each of next 21 dc; repeat from * twice, 3 sc in next corner tr, sc in remaining 10 dc, sl st in first sc to join—96 sc.

Fasten off. Weave in the ends.

Square Backing

With yarn B, ch 28, turn.

NOTE: *To make joining the squares easier, work the first row into the bottom side of the foundation chain, inserting the hook into the loop of each stitch with the V of the stitch below your hook.*

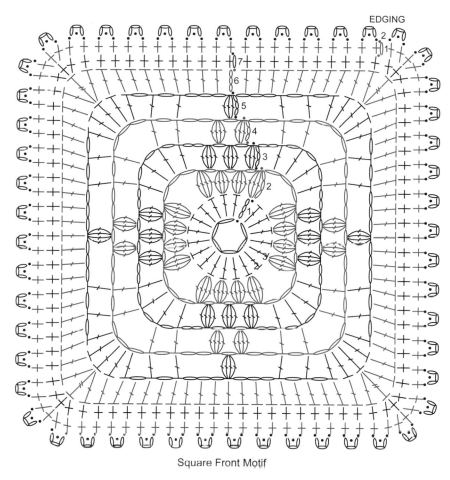

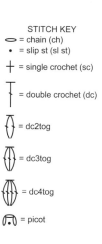

Square Front Motif

STITCH KEY
- ⌒ = chain (ch)
- • = slip st (sl st)
- ✝ = single crochet (sc)
- ┬ = double crochet (dc)
- ⧅ = dc2tog
- ⧉ = dc3tog
- ⧊ = dc4tog
- ⌒✝ = picot

ROW 1 (RS) Sc in 2nd ch from hook, sc in each ch across, turn—27 sc.

ROWS 2–29 Ch 1, sc in each sc across, turn—27 sc.

ROW 30 Ch 1, sc in each sc across—27 sc.

Fasten off. Weave in the ends. Block the motif and the backing to measure 7½" (19cm) by 7½" (19cm).

Edging

ROUND 1 (RS—JOINING ROUND): With wrong sides facing, holding the two squares together, matching corner stitches, join the two pieces together. With right side facing you, working through double thickness, join yarn A in any stitch on outer edge of trivet, ch 1, sc in each stitch around, except work 3 sc in each corner stitch, sl st in first sc to join.

ROUND 2 *Ch 3, sl st in 3rd ch from hook (picot made), sl st in each of next 2 sc; repeat from * around, ending with sl st in first sl st to join.

Fasten off. Weave in the ends.

ROUND TRIVET

Round Front Motif

With yarn C, ch 8, join with a sl st to form a ring.

ROUND 1 (RS) Ch 1, 12 sc into ring, sl st in first sc to join—12 sc.

ROUND 2 Ch 3, dc in same stitch (counts as dc2tog), ch 3, (dc2tog, ch 3) in each sc around, sl st to top of beginning ch to join—12 ch-3 lps.

ROUND 3 Sl st to center of first ch-3 lp, ch 1, (sc, ch 4) in each ch-3 lp around, sl st in first sc to join—12 ch-4 lps.

ROUND 4 Sl st in next ch-4 lp, ch 1, (2 sc, ch 3, 2 sc) in each ch-4 lp around, sl st to first sc to join—12 ch-3 lps.

ROUND 5 Sl st to next ch-3 lp, ch 3, dc2tog in first ch-3 lp (counts as dc3tog), ch 4, dc3tog in same ch-3 lp, (dc3tog, ch 4, dc3tog) in each ch-3 lp around, sl st in first cluster to join—24 dc3tog; 12 ch-4 lps.

ROUND 6 Ch 1, sc in first cluster, *5 sc in next ch-4 sp, sk next cluster, sc in next cluster; repeat from * around, omitting last sc, sl st in first sc to join—72 sc.

ROUND 7 Ch 4 (counts as tr), dc in next 5 sc, *tr in next sc, dc in next 5 sc; repeat from * around, sl st in top of beginning ch to join—72 stitches.

ROUND 8 Ch 1, 2 sc in first stitch, sc in each of next 5 dc, *2 sc in next tr, sc in each of next 5 dc; repeat from * around, sl st in first sc to join—84 sc.

Fasten off. Weave in the ends.

Round Backing
NOTE: *The backing is worked in spiral crochet where rounds are not joined.*

With yarn D, make a magic ring.
ROUND 1 (RS) Ch 1, 6 sc in ring, do not join—6 sc. Place a stitch marker in the last stitch, and move marker up to each new round as you proceed to mark where to begin each subsequent round.

ROUND 2 Work 2 sc in each sc around—12 sc.

ROUND 3 *Sc in next sc, 2 sc in next sc; repeat from * around—18 sc.

ROUND 4 *Sc in next 2 sc, 2 sc in next sc; repeat from * around—24 sc.

ROUND 5 *Sc in next 3 sc, 2 sc in next sc; repeat from * around—30 sc.

ROUND 6 *Sc in next 4 sc, 2 sc in next sc; repeat from * around—36 sc.

ROUND 7 *Sc in next 5 sc, 2 sc in next sc; repeat from * around—42 sc.

ROUND 8 *Sc in next 6 sc, 2 sc in next sc; repeat from * around—48 sc.

ROUND 9 *Sc in next 7 sc, 2 sc in next sc; repeat from * around—54 sc.

ROUND 10 *Sc in next 8 sc, 2 sc in next sc; repeat from * around—60 sc.

ROUND 11 *Sc in next 9 sc, 2 sc in next sc; repeat from * around—66 sc.

ROUND 12 *Sc in next 10 sc, 2 sc in next sc; repeat from * around—72 sc.

ROUND 13 *Sc in next 11 sc, 2 sc in next sc; repeat from * around, sl st in first sc to join—78 sc.

Fasten off. Weave in the ends.

EDGING

Round Front Motif

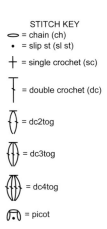

STITCH KEY

- ⌒ = chain (ch)
- • = slip st (sl st)
- ┼ = single crochet (sc)
- ┬ = double crochet (dc)
- ⧫ = dc2tog
- ⧫ = dc3tog
- ⧫ = dc4tog
- ⌒ꓹ⌒ = picot

Block the front motif and the backing to the same size.

Edging

ROUND 1 (RS—JOINING ROUND)
With wrong sides facing, hold the two circles together with the right side of the *Round Front Motif* facing you and join the two pieces together. Working through double thickness, join yarn A in any stitch on outer edge of trivet, ch 1, then sc in each sc around, sl st in first sc to join.

ROUND 2 Ch 3, sl st in 3rd ch from hook (picot made), sl st in each of next 2 sc; repeat from * around, ending with sl st in first sl st to join.

FINISHING (OPTIONAL)

To make the motifs more pronounced, hand-tack the motif to the backing using thread that matches the backing. Bring the needle up through the backing square (or circle) and pass it through the backside of a few stitches in the motif, then draw the thread back through the backing square, being careful to make stitches invisible. Continue sewing through the motif until you work your way around the entire design.

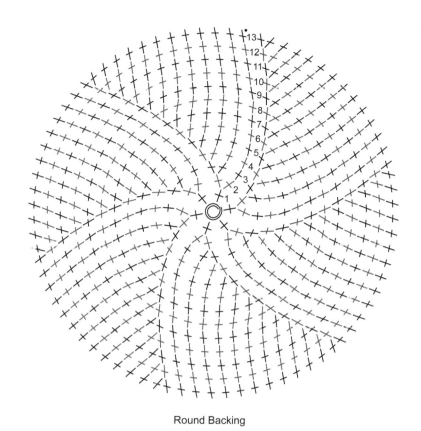

Round Backing

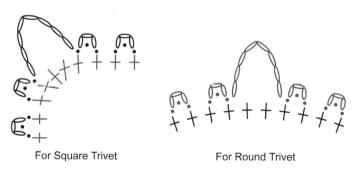

TIP: If you'd like to make a hanging loop on your trivet, stop the edging pattern just before any corner on the square or anywhere on the circle, ch 8, sk 3 stitches, then continue with the edging pattern in the next stitch.

For Square Trivet   For Round Trivet

Butterfly Apron

Add a dainty touch to your favorite apron with a delicate pocket and trim. Working this trim is easy because it doesn't require a lengthy foundation chain—you work the pattern as you go, ensuring the perfect measurements. Instructions for sewing your own apron are included.

Skill Level **Advanced**

Finished Measurements

Pocket measures 8" (20.5cm) wide by 5½" (14cm) tall. Trim measures 1½" (4cm) wide. Finished apron (optional) measures 32" (81.5cm) wide by 17½" (44.5cm) long.

Materials

- 1 ball of J&P Coats *Royale Fashion Crochet #3*, 100% mercerized cotton, 150 yd (137m), #0625 Sage **1**
- Size 5 (1.90mm) steel crochet hook, or size to obtain gauge
- Stitch markers
- Yarn needle
- T-pins, iron, and blocking board
- Apron to embellish or materials to make apron (see *Sewing the Apron*)
- Straight pins
- Sewing machine or hand-sewing needle
- Matching sewing thread

Gauge

Gauge is not critical for this project. Two repeats of trim worked for Rows 1 and 2 measures 4" (10cm) long and 1⅜" (3.5cm) wide. First 2 rounds of Small Circle measures 1⅝" (4cm) in diameter.

Special Stitches

3 TREBLE CLUSTER (3-tr cluster) (Yo twice, insert hook in next stitch, yo, draw yarn through stitch, [yo, draw yarn through 2 lps on hook] twice) 3 times in same stitch, yo, draw yarn through 4 lps on hook.

PUFF STITCH (Yo, insert hook in BL of stitch indicated, yo, draw yarn through stitch) 3 times in same stitch, yo, draw through 7 lps on hook.

PICOT Ch 3, sc in 3rd ch from hook.

TRIM

NOTE: *Make the trim in a length to match the bottom edge of your apron. If you're sewing the included apron pattern, your trim should measure 32" (81.5cm) long.*

Ch 10.

ROW 1 (RS) *3-tr cluster in 10th ch from hook, (ch 5, puff stitch in 5th ch from hook) twice, ch 10; repeat from * until trim reaches desired length. Fasten off, leaving a long end to weave in.

ROW 2 With right side facing, join yarn in ch at base of first 3-tr cluster, sl st in next ch-10 lp, ch 7 (counts as first tr, ch 3), sc in 3rd ch from hook for picot, (tr, picot) 6 times in same ch-9 lp, tr in same ch-9 lp, *sc in each of next 2 ch-4 lps, (tr, picot) 6 times in next ch-9 lp, tr in same ch-9 lp; repeat from * across. Fasten off. Weave in the ends.

BUTTERFLY POCKET

NOTE: *The pocket is made in three sections—the butterfly body and two wings. Each wing is made up of a Small Circle and a Large Circle, which are then sewn together and edged. To better understand the construction, read through all of the instructions and refer to the diagram before you begin.*

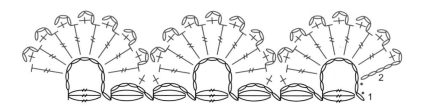

STITCH KEY

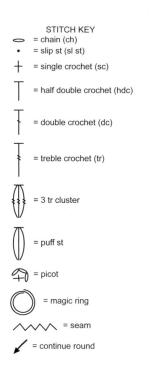

- ⬭ = chain (ch)
- • = slip st (sl st)
- + = single crochet (sc)
- T = half double crochet (hdc)
- ⊥ = double crochet (dc)
- ⊥ = treble crochet (tr)
- = 3 tr cluster
- = puff st
- = picot
- ◯ = magic ring
- ⋀⋀⋀ = seam
- ↙ = continue round

Butterfly Body

Ch 30.

ROUND 1 (RS) Dc in 4th ch from hook, dc in each of next 25 ch, 5 dc in last ch, working across opposite side of foundation ch, dc in each of next 26 ch, 4 dc in next ch, sl st in top of beginning ch to join—62 dc.

Fasten off yarn and weave in the ends.

Butterfly Wings

Work two Small Circles—you'll need one for each wing. Next, follow the instructions for the Large Circle, making two. Note that the wing edging is shaped differently for the left and right wings of the butterfly; be sure to make one left and one right wing.

SMALL CIRCLE (MAKE 2)

Make a magic ring.

ROUND 1 (RS) Ch 4 (counts as first dc, ch 1 here and throughout), *dc in ring, ch 1; repeat from * 8 times more, sl st in top of beginning ch to join—10 ch-1 sps.

ROUND 2 Ch 3 (counts as first dc here and throughout), dc in first stitch, ch 2, *2 dc in next dc, ch 2; repeat from * around, sl st in top of beginning ch to join—10 ch-2 spaces.

Fasten off, leaving a 10" (25.5cm) tail.

LARGE CIRCLE (MAKE 2)

Make a magic ring.

ROUND 1 (RS) Ch 4, *dc in ring, ch 1; repeat from * 8 times, sl st in top of beginning ch to join—10 ch-1 sps.

ROUND 2 Ch 3, dc in first st, 2 dc in next ch-1 sp, *2 dc in next dc, 2 dc in next ch-1 sp; repeat from * around, sl st in top of beginning ch to join—40 dc.

ROUND 3 Ch 5 (counts as first dc, ch 2), sk next dc, *dc in next dc, ch 2, sk next dc; repeat from * around, sl st in top of beginning ch to join—20 ch-2 sps. **DO NOT FASTEN OFF**, continue to Right Wing Edging or Left Wing Edging.

RIGHT WING EDGING (CONTINUE WORKING INTO ONE LARGE CIRCLE)

ROUND E1 Ch 2 (counts as first hdc), 3 hdc in next ch-2 sp, *hdc in next dc, 3 hdc in next ch-2 sp*; repeat from * to * 5 times; dc in next dc, 3 tr in next ch-2 sp, ch 3, sc in 3rd ch from hook (picot), 3 tr in next ch-2 sp, dc in next dc, 3 hdc in next ch-2 sp; repeat from * to * 10 times, sl st in top of beginning ch to join—80 stitches. **DO NOT FASTEN OFF**. Drop yarn to be picked up later—insert a latching stitch marker in the dropped loop to keep your work from unraveling.

Using the 10" (25.5cm) tail from the Small Circle, sew the first 8 stitches of the Small Circle to the first 9 stitches of the last round of the Large Circle (see diagram).

CONTINUE ROUND E1 Pick up the dropped loop at the end of Round 1, *hdc in next 2 dc of Small Circle, 3 hdc in next ch-2 sp*; repeat from

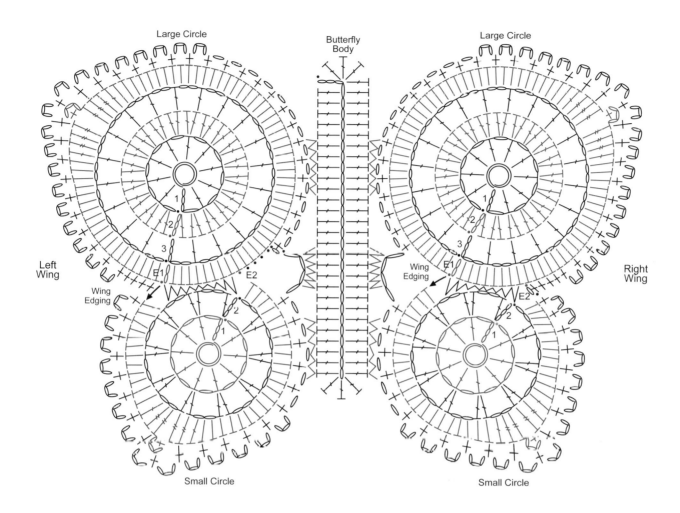

Large Circle

Butterfly
Body

Large Circle

Left
Wing

Wing
Edging

E1

E2

Wing
Edging

E1

E2

Right
Wing

Small Circle

Small Circle

* to * 3 times, hdc in next 2 dc, (dc, 2 tr) in next ch-2 sp, ch 3, sc in 3rd ch from hook (picot), tr in next 2 dc, (dc, 2 hdc) in next ch-3 sp; repeat from * to * twice more, sl st in next hdc on Large Circle.

ROUND E2 Ch 1, sc in first 5 stitches, *ch 3, sk next stitch, sc in next stitch *; treating picot as 1 stitch, repeat from * to * 17 times more, **ch 1, sk next stitch, sc in next stitch **; repeat from ** to ** 12 times more, ch 4, sk next 5 stitches on Large Circle, sk next 3 stitches on Small Circle, sc in next stitch, repeat from ** to ** 5 times more, treating picot

as 1 stitch, repeat from * to * 14 times more.

Fasten off.

The Large Circle is the top of the wing.

LEFT WING EDGING (CONTINUE WORKING INTO ONE LARGE CIRCLE)

ROUND E1 Ch 2, 3 hdc in next ch-2 sp, *hdc in next dc, 3 hdc in ch 2 sp*; repeat from * to * 12 times more, dc in next dc, 3 tr in next ch-2 sp, ch 3, sc in 3rd ch from hook (picot), 3 tr in next ch-2 sp, dc in next dc, 3 hdc in next ch-2 sp; repeat from * to * 4

times more; sl st in top of beginning ch to join. **DO NOT FASTEN OFF.** Drop yarn to be picked up later—insert a stitch marker in the dropped loop to keep your work from unraveling.

Using the 10" (25.5cm) tail from the Small Circle, sew the first 8 stitches of the Small Circle to the first 9 stitches of the last round of the Large Circle (see diagram).

CONTINUE ROUND E1 Pick up the dropped loop at the end of Round 1, *hdc in next 2 dc of Small Circle, 3 hdc in next ch-2 sp*; repeat from * to * once more, dc in next 2 dc, (dc, 2 tr) in next ch-2 sp, ch 3, sc in 3rd ch from hook (picot), tr in next 2 dc, (dc, 2 hdc) in next ch-2 sp; repeat from * to * 4 times more, sl st in next hdc of Large Circle.

ROUND E2 Sl st through the next 5 hdc, (ch 1, sc) in next stitch, *ch 1, sk next stitch, sc in next stitch*; repeat from * to * 12 times more, **ch 3, sk next stitch, sc in next stitch**; treating picot as 1 stitch, repeat from ** to ** 17 times more, sc in next 4 stitches, sc in next stitch of Small Circle; treating picot as 1 stitch, repeat from ** to ** 14 times more, repeat from * to * 5 times more; ch 4, sl st in first sc to join.

Fasten off.

The Large Circle is the top of the wing.

ASSEMBLING BUTTERFLY POCKET

Block the butterfly pieces and let them dry.

With right sides facing, align the inner left wing edge with the left body edge. Referring to the diagram, sew the wing to the body in sections with one long strand of crochet thread. Make about six whipstitches on the small circle edge, three stitches in the ch-4 lp, and eight in the large circle edge of the wing, weaving the yarn through backside of the butterfly body between stitches. Repeat this process for the right wing, and then weave in all of the remaining yarn ends.

FINISHING

Block trim. Pin the trim to the bottom edge of your apron as shown in the photo or as desired. Machine or hand-sew the trim to the apron along the cluster and puff stitch edge.

Pin the butterfly pocket in place as desired. Machine or hand-sew around the sides and bottom of the butterfly, being careful to make small, invisible stitches.

Sewing the Apron (*optional*)

Materials

- ½ yd (46cm) 45"- (114cm) wide cotton (main fabric)
- ⅔ yd (61cm) contrasting fabric (for hem and ties)
- Scissors or rotary cutter and quilting ruler
- Straight pins
- Iron
- Sewing machine
- Thread
- Bodkin or safety pin

NOTE: *Use a ½" (13mm) seam allowance throughout.*

Cut one 16" (40.5cm) x 35" (89cm) rectangle from the main fabric; this will be the apron body.

From the contrasting fabric, cut one 8" (20.5cm) by 35" (89cm) rectangle (for the hem), one 6" (15cm) by 22" (56cm) rectangle (for the waistband) and two 6" (15cm) by 30" (76cm) rectangles (for the ties).

APRON BODY

With right sides facing, match the 35" (89cm) apron body edge to the 35" (89cm) edge of the hem rectangle. Pin the pieces in place and sew the seam. Press the seam toward the bottom of the apron.

Fold the short sides of the apron under 1" (2.5cm) and press. Fold the pressed fold under ½" (13mm) and press again. Working on the back of the apron, fold the bottom hem strip up so that 1" (2.5cm) of the contrasting material overlaps the seam you just sewed. Press the fold at the bottom of the apron. Fold the raw edge of the hem strip under ½" (13mm) and press. Pin the contrasting hem edge in place on the back side of the apron, using the seam as a guide. Pin the folded sides of the apron in place. Starting at the right side of the apron and removing the pins as you go, sew down one short side, across the bottom and back up the other short side of the apron. Next, sew across the top of the contrasting hem, being sure to catch the fold on the back of the apron. Press the piece.

TIES AND WAISTBAND

Fold both apron tie rectangles in half lengthwise, matching long edges and with the right sides of the fabric facing, and press the fold. Stitch down the long raw edge of each tie to form a fabric tube. Use the bodkin or safety pin to turn the fabric tubes inside out, and press. Press one short end of each tie under ½" (13mm) and sew shut.

With the wrong sides facing, fold the waistband piece in half lengthwise and press. Fold one long edge and both of the short edges under ½" (13mm) and press.

FINISHING APRON

Baste the top of the apron with long, gathering stitches. Do **NOT** back stitch at the beginning or end of your basting seam, and leave your thread ends long at both the beginning and end of the seam. Pull the thread ends to gather up the stitches on the top edge of your apron until it measures 21" (53.5cm) wide. Knot both long ends of the basting thread to hold the gathers in place.

Next, pin the wrong side of the gathered apron edge to the right side of the waistband (the un-pressed edge). Stitch the pieces together and press the stitched edge toward the waistband. Fold the pressed long edge of the waistband over the apron top and pin it in place, making sure to catch the entire gathered apron edge underneath the waistband. Place the raw ends of the apron ties about ½" (13mm) inside the waistband on either side and pin them in place. Sew around the entire waistband, removing the pins as you go, and be sure to catch the ties and the gathered apron top in your seam.

Attach the embellishments as directed above.

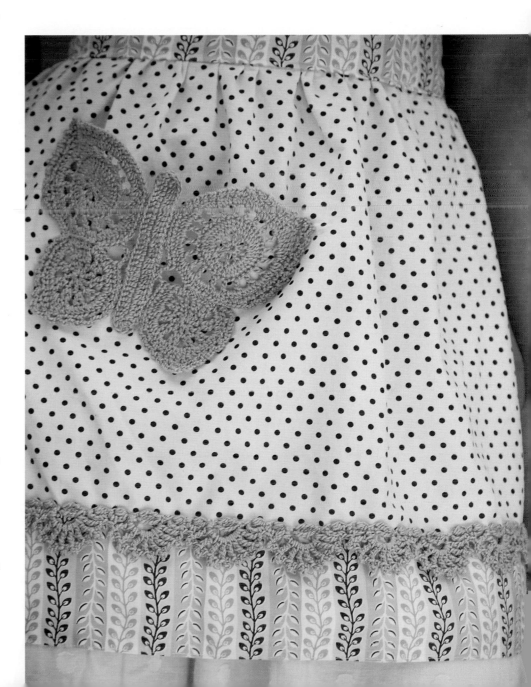

Medallion Table Mat

Why wait for a special occasion? Dress up your dining table with a sweet crocheted table mat. The flower-like medallions are quick to stitch, and durable cotton yarn ensures that you can use it over and over again. If you're having a party, whip up some extra motifs to use as matching coasters.

Skill Level **Easy**

Finished Measurements

Completed piece measures 39" (99cm) long by 15" (38cm) wide. To alter the length or width, adjust the number and arrangement of the medallions.

Materials

- 1 ball each of Lion Brand *Lion Cotton*, 100% cotton, 236 yd (212m), 5 oz (140g), in #140 Rose (A), #180 Evergreen (B), and #123 Seaspray (C) 4
- Size F-5 (3.75mm) crochet hook, or size to obtain gauge
- Yarn needle
- T-pins, iron, and blocking board

Gauge

Small motif worked through Round 3 measures 3" (7.5cm) in diameter.

SMALL MEDALLION (MAKE 8)

With yarn A, ch 8, join with a sl st to form a ring.

ROUND 1 (RS) Ch 1, 12 sc in ring, sl st in first sc to join—12 sc.

ROUND 2 Ch 4 (counts as dc, ch 1), (dc, ch 1) in each dc around, sl st in 3rd ch of beginning ch to join—12 ch-1 sps.

ROUND 3 Ch 3, 2 dc in next ch-1 sp, *dc in next dc, 2 dc in next ch-1 sp; repeat from * around, sl st in top of beginning ch to join—36 dc.

ROUND 4 Ch 1, sc in first stitch, ch 4, sk next dc, *sc in next dc, ch 4, sk next dc; repeat from * around, sl st in first sc to join—18 ch-4 lps.

Fasten off, leaving a 12" (30.5cm) tail for joining medallions. Weave in the center end.

MEDIUM MEDALLION (MAKE 6)

With yarn B, make a magic ring.

ROUND 1 (RS) Ch 3 (counts as dc), 11 dc in ring, sl st in top of beginning ch to join—12 dc.

ROUND 2 Ch 1, sc in first stitch, ch 5, sk next dc, *sc in next dc, ch 5, sk next dc; repeat from * around, sl st in first sc to join—6 ch-5 lps.

ROUND 3 Ch 5 (counts as dc, ch 2), sc in next ch-5 lp, ch 2, *dc in next sc, ch 2, sc in next ch-5 lp, ch 2; repeat from * around, sl st in 3rd ch of beginning ch to join—12 ch-2 sps.

ROUND 4 *5 dc in next sc, sl st in next dc; repeat from * around, ending with sl st in first stitch to join—6 shells.

ROUND 5 Ch 8 (counts as tr, ch 4), sk next 2 dc, hdc in next dc, ch 4, sk next 2 dc, *tr in next sl st, ch 4, sk next 2 dc, hdc in next dc, ch 4, sk next 2 dc; repeat from * around, sl st in 4th ch of turning ch to join—12 ch-4 lps.

ROUND 6 *Ch 1, 4 dc in 2nd ch of next ch-4 lp, ch 1, sl st in next hdc, ch 1, 4 dc in 2nd ch of next ch-4 lp, ch 1, sl st in next tr; repeat from * around, ending with last sl st in first stitch to join—12 shells.

Fasten off, leaving a 12" (30.5cm) tail for joining medallions. Weave in the center end.

LARGE MEDALLION (MAKE 5)

With yarn C, make a magic ring.

ROUND 1 (RS) Ch 3 (counts as dc), 7 dc in ring, sl st in top of beginning ch to join—8 dc.

ROUND 2 Ch 3 (counts as hdc, ch 1), (hdc, ch 1) in each dc around, sl st in 2nd ch of beginning ch to join—8 ch-1 sps.

ROUND 3 Sl st in first ch-1 sp, ch 1, (sc, ch 4) in each ch-1 sp around, ending with ch 2, hdc in first sc instead of last ch-4 lp (this will put the yarn in the correct position to begin the next round)—8 lps.

ROUND 4 Ch 1, (sc, ch 5) in each lp around, ending with ch-2, dc in first sc instead of last ch-5 lp to join—8 ch-5 lps.

ROUND 5 Ch 1, (sc, ch 6) in each lp around, ending with sl st in first sc to join—8 ch-6 lps.

ROUND 6 Ch 3, 3 dc (counts as 4 dc, shell made) in first sc, ch 2, sc in next ch-6 lp, ch 2, *4 dc in next sc, ch 2, sc in next ch-6 lp, ch 2; repeat from * around, sl st in top of beginning ch to join—8 shells.

ROUND 7 Sl st to 3rd dc of next shell, ch 1, sc in same dc, *ch 5, sk next ch-2 sp, sc in next sc, ch 5, sk next 2 dc, sc in next dc; repeat from * around, ending with ch-3, dc in first sc instead of last ch-5 lp to join—16 ch-5 lps.

ROUND 8 Ch 1, (sc, ch 6) in each lp around, ending with ch-3, dc in first sc instead of last ch-6 lp to join—16 ch-6 lps.

ROUND 9 Ch 1, sc in first lp, (2 dc, ch 2, 2 dc) in next sc (shell made),

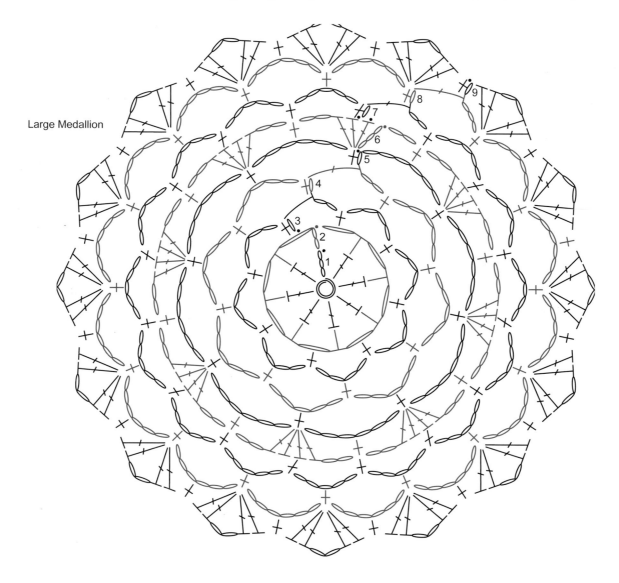

Large Medallion

*sc in next ch-6 lp, (2 dc, ch 2, 2 dc) in next sc; repeat from * around, sl st in first sc to join—16 shells.

Fasten off, leaving a 12" (30.5cm) tail for joining medallions. Weave in the center end.

FINISHING

Block all of the medallions and let them dry. Place the medallions together as shown in the construction diagram, then join them with a whipstitch through the back loops of each medallion. To make it easy, sew a few medallions together in sections, then join the sections together. Weave in any remaining ends.

DIAGRAM KEY
S = Small Medallion
M = Medium Medallion
L = Large Medallion

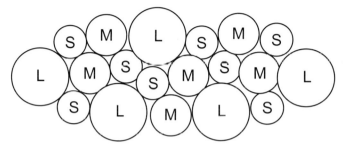

Construction Diagram

Medium Medallion

Small Medallion

STITCH KEY

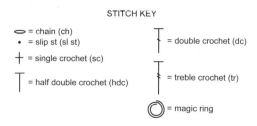

= chain (ch)
= slip st (sl st)
= single crochet (sc)
= half double crochet (hdc)
= double crochet (dc)
= treble crochet (tr)
= magic ring

Lace Bowl

Doilies aren't just for collecting dust anymore. Make up a whole set of doily-inspired dishes for a charming display. This bowl is perfect for holding fruit, candies, or even your current fiber of choice. Try crocheting this pattern with different yarn weights for a range of sizes. Use commercial fabric stiffener or a basic sugar and water solution to set the bowl's shape.

Skill Level **Intermediate**

Finished Size

Before shaping the crochet over a bowl form, the bowl's diameter is 11½" (29cm), unstretched.

Materials

- 1 skein of Brown Sheep *Cotton Fine,* 80% cotton, 20% merino wool, 222 yd (203m), 1¾ oz (50g), #100 Cotton Ball 🌀
- Size C-2 (2.75mm) crochet hook, or size to obtain gauge
- Yarn needle
- 2 cups (480ml) sugar, 1 cup (240ml) water, 2 qt. (1.9l) saucepan and tongs *or* commercial fabric stiffener
- One large mixing bowl (for bowl form), approximately 10" (25.5cm) in diameter
- Plastic wrap
- Kraft paper or newspaper

Gauge

First 6 rounds of pattern worked measures 3¼" (8.5cm) in diameter.

Special Stitches

DOUBLE CROCHET 2 TOGETHER DECREASE (dc2tog)
(Yo, insert hook in next stitch, yo, draw yarn through stitch, yo, draw yarn through 2 lps on hook) twice, yo, draw yarn through 3 lps on hook.

DOUBLE CROCHET 3 TOGETHER DECREASE (dc3tog)
(Yo, insert hook in next stitch, yo, draw yarn through stitch, yo, draw yarn through 2 lps on hook) 3 times, yo, draw yarn through 4 lps on hook.

BOWL

Make a magic ring.

ROUND 1 (RS) Ch 1, 12 sc in ring—12 sc.

ROUND 2 Ch 1, sc in first sc, *ch 5, sk 1 sc, sc in next sc; repeat from * 4 times, ending with ch 2, dc in first sc of round (counts as ch-5 lp and puts yarn in the correct position to start next round)—6 ch-5 lps.

ROUND 3 Ch 3 (counts as dc here and throughout), 4 dc in first lp, ch 5, *5 dc in next ch-5 lp, ch 5; repeat from * around, sl st in top of beginning ch to join—6 ch-5 lps.

ROUND 4 Ch 3, dc in next 4 dc, ch 3, sc in next ch-5 sp, ch 3, *dc in next 5 dc, ch 3, sc in next ch-5 lp, ch 3; repeat from * around, sl st in top of beginning ch to join—12 ch-3 lps.

ROUND 5 Ch 3, dc in next dc (counts as dc2tog), dc in next dc, dc2tog in next 2 dc, (ch 4, sc) in each of next 2 ch-3 lps, ch 4, *dc2tog in next 2 dc, dc in next dc, dc2tog in next 2 dc, (ch 4, sc) in each of next 2 ch-3 lps, ch 4; repeat from * around, sl st in top of beginning ch to join—18 ch-4 lps.

ROUND 6 Ch 3, dc2tog in next 2 dc (counts as dc3tog), (ch 5, sc) in each of next 3 ch-4 lps, ch 5, *dc3tog in next 3 dc, (ch 5, sc) in each of next 3 ch-4 lps, ch 5; repeat from * around, ending with ch 2, dc in top of beginning ch instead of last ch-5 lp—24 ch-5 lps.

ROUND 7 Ch 1, sc in first lp, ch 6, (sc, ch 6) in each ch-5 lp around, sl st in first sc to join—24 ch-5 lps.

ROUND 8 Sl st in next ch-5 lp, ch 3, (2 dc, ch 2, 3 dc) in first ch-5 lp (shell made), sc in next lp, *(3 dc, ch 2, 3 dc) in next ch-5 lp, sc in next lp; repeat from * around, sl st

in top of beginning ch to join—12 shells; 12 sc.

ROUND 9 Ch 3, dc in next 2 dc, ch 1, dc in next 3 dc, ch 6, sk next (sc, dc), sc in next dc, ch 6, sk next (dc, ch 2, dc), sc in next dc, ch 6, sk next (dc, sc), *dc in next 3 dc, ch 1, dc in next 3 dc, ch 6, sk next (dc, ch 2, dc), sc in next dc, ch 6, sk next (dc, sc); repeat from * around, sl st in top of beginning ch to join—18 ch-6 lps.

ROUND 10 Ch 3, dc in next 2 dc, sk next ch-1 sp, dc in next 3 dc, (ch 4, sc) in each of next 3 ch-6 lps, ch 4, *dc in next 3 dc, sk next ch-1 sp, dc in next 3 dc, (ch 4, sc) in each of next 3 ch-6 lps, ch 4; repeat from * around, sl st in top of beginning ch to join—24 ch-6 lps.

ROUND 11 Ch 3, (dc2tog in next 2 dc) twice, dc in next dc, (ch 5, sc) in each of next 4 ch-4 lps, ch 5, *dc in next dc, (dc2tog in next 2 dc) twice, dc in next dc, (ch 5, sc) in each of next 4 ch-4 lps, ch 5; repeat from * around, sl st in top of beginning ch to join—30 ch-6 lps.

ROUND 12 Ch 3, dc2tog in next 2 dc, dc in next dc, (ch 5, sc) in each of next 5 ch-4 lps, ch 5, *dc in next dc, dc2tog in next 2 dc, dc in next dc, (ch 5, sc) in each of next 5 ch-4 lps , ch 5; repeat from * around, sl st in top of beginning ch to join—36 ch-6 lps.

ROUND 13 Sl st in next st, ch 1, sc in same st, (ch 5, sc) in each of next 6 ch-5 lps, *ch 5, sk next dc, sc in next st, (ch 5, sc) in each of next 6 ch-5 lps; repeat from * around, ending

with ch 2, dc in first sc instead of last ch-5 lp—42 ch-5 lps.

ROUNDS 14–15 Ch 1, sc in first lp, (ch 5, sc) in each ch-5 lp around, ending with ch 2, dc in first sc instead of last ch-5 lp—42 ch-5 lps.

ROUND 16 Ch 1, sc in first lp, (ch 4, sc) in each ch-5 lp around, ending with ch 4, sl st in first sc to join—42 ch-4 lps.

ROUND 17 Sl st in first ch-4 lp, ch 3, 3 dc in first ch-4 lp, 4 dc in each ch-4 lp around, sl st in top of beginning ch to join 168 dc.

ROUND 18 Sk first 2 dc, (3 dc in next dc, ch 1, 3 dc in next dc) (shell made), sk next dc, sl st in next dc, *sl st in next dc, sk next dc, 3 dc in next dc, ch 1, 3 dc in next dc, sk next dc, sl st in next dc; repeat from * around, sl st in first sl st to join—28 shells.

ROUND 19 Ch 6 (counts as dc, ch 3), sc in next ch-1 sp, ch 3, dc between next 2 sl sts, *ch 3, sc in next ch-1 sp, ch 3, dc between next 2 sl sts, repeat from * around, ending with ch 3, sc in next ch-1 sp, ch 3, sl st in 3rd ch of beginning ch to join—56 ch-3 lps.

ROUND 20 *Ch 3, sk next ch-3 sp, (dc, ch 3, dc) in next sc (V-st made), ch 3, sk next ch-3 sp, sl st in next 9 stitches; repeat from * around, omitting last 4 sl sts, ending with sl st in last sc—28 V-stitches.

ROUND 21 Sk next ch-3 sp of round 19, *5 dc in each of next 3 ch-3 sps (fan made), sk next 4 sl sts, sc in next sl st (above sc from round 19); repeat from * around, sl st in first dc to join—28 fans.

Fasten off. Weave in the ends.

FINISHING

Before you stiffen the piece, drape it over some of the bowls in your cupboard to get a feel for your ideal bowl shape. Using a tall, narrow

MAKE THE STARCH ▪ ● ▪ ●

Place two cups of sugar and one cup of water in a saucepan. Stir the mixture constantly and heat it on the stove just until the sugar dissolves. Be very careful, as the solution is hot! Remove the pan from the heat and soak the crocheted bowl in the solution, using tongs to make sure the bowl is saturated. Let the solution cool slightly. With the tongs, remove the crocheted bowl from the saucepan, squeezing it as much as possible to remove any excess solution. Drape it over the bowl form, stretching it into shape with the tongs as desired. You can further shape the crocheted bowl with your fingers in a few minutes when the piece has cooled somewhat. Let the bowl dry for three days or until it is hard. Once the yarn returns to its original color, the bowl is starched and ready for use.

bowl as a form will yield a bowl that ruffles at the top, while a wider bowl creates a shallow dish-like shape.

To stiffen your bowl, you can use a commercial stiffener or a trusty homemade recipe of sugar and water (see *Make the Starch*). The solution takes quite a while to dry (count on at least three days), but you'll be surprised how well it works. If you want to use a commercial stiffener, try Aleene's Fabric Stiffener and Draping Liquid and follow the package instructions.

If you're using the homemade solution, cover your work surface with plastic wrap or a garbage bag, then cover this with several sheets of kraft paper or newspaper—the sugar mixture will be very sticky. Cover the bowl you are using in plastic wrap to make cleanup easier. Place the wrapped bowl upside down on top of the kraft paper, and follow the instructions in *Make the Starch*.

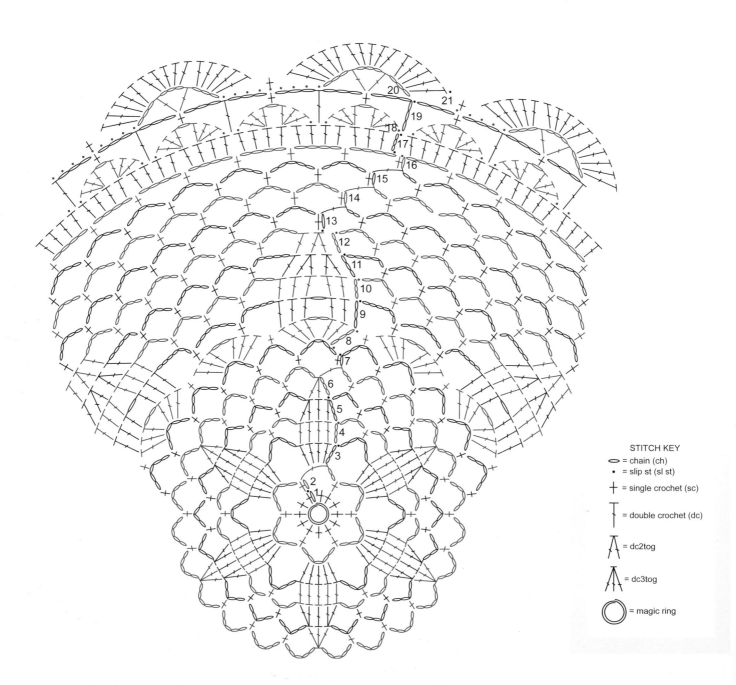

STITCH KEY

◯ = chain (ch)

• = slip st (sl st)

+ = single crochet (sc)

T = double crochet (dc)

⋀ = dc2tog

⋀ = dc3tog

◯ = magic ring

Stitch
Dictionary

Trims

Crocheted trims look great on everything from baby blankets to summer skirts—whether you crocheted, knit, sewed, or purchased the original item. Although the trims in this book are designed to stand alone so that they can be sewn to readymade garments, many of these patterns can also be used as edgings by working them directly into the edge of a crocheted or knit item. Look for a trim that's worked in rows and refer to the diagram to figure out where exactly the decoration starts—generally, you can skip the foundation chain and the first row of single or double crochet (if you prefer), and then work the stitch combinations right into the edge of your piece.

Loops and Circles

Chain Loops

ROW 1 (RS) Ch 5, dc in 5th ch from hook, *ch 6, dc in 5th ch from hook; repeat from * until trim measures desired length.
ROW 2 Ch 1, turn work to the dc side of Row 1, *2 sc around the post of next dc, sc in next ch; repeat from * across, turn.
ROW 3 Ch 1, sc in each sc across. Fasten off.

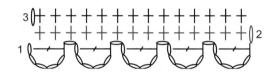

STITCH KEY
⬯ = chain (ch)

+ = single crochet (sc)

T = double crochet (dc)

Chain Links

ROUND 1 (RS) *Ch 3, 4 sc in 2nd ch from hook; repeat from * 6 times, ch 3, 8 sc in 2nd ch from hook. Working across opposite side, sl st in 8th sc from hook, **sl st in next sc, 4 sc in 2nd ch of next ch-3, sk 2 sc from opposite side and sl st in next sc, repeat from ** across row, ending with sc in first ch of round. Fasten off.

STITCH KEY
◯ or ⬯ = chain (ch)

• = slip stitch (sl st)

+ = single crochet (sc)

↑ = direction to next st

Here are a few ways to have fun with trims:

- Try making each row in a different color for a funky look.
- Add rows of single, double, or half double crochet right after working the foundation chain to make a wider trim.

- For trims worked in rows, try working the same pattern on both sides of the foundation chain for an insertion or double-edged trim.

- For a nice straight edge, work the foundation row into the bottom loop of the chain (so that the V is under your hook).
- Remember to block your trims for the best results!

Sideways Loops

ROW 1 (RS) Ch 7, tr in 7th ch from hook, *ch 11, tr in 7th ch from hook; repeat from * until trim measures desired length, ch 5.
ROW 2 Working in tr side of Row 1, sc in 2nd ch from hook, sc in each of next 3 ch, *3 sc around the post of next tr**, sc in each of next 4 ch; repeat from * across, ending last repeat at **.

ROW 3 Sl st in first ch of Row 1, ch 1, turn back to the top of Row 1, *(sl st, ch 1, 3 sc, 2 dc, tr) in ch-6 lp**, sk next 4 ch, sl st in next ch at base of tr; repeat from * across, ending last repeat at **, sk next 3 ch, sl st in next ch. Fasten off.

STITCH KEY
⌒ = chain (ch)
• = slip st (sl st)
+ = single crochet (sc)
T = double crochet (dc)
⊤ = treble crochet (tr)

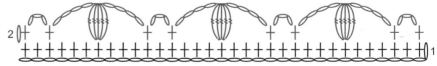

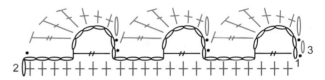

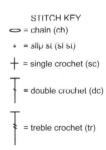

Bobble Loops

TREBLE 5 TOGETHER (bobble) (Yo twice, insert hook in stitch, yo, draw yarn through stitch, [yo, draw yarn through 2 lps on hook] twice) 5 times in same stitch, yo, draw yarn through 6 lps on hook.

Ch a multiple of 10 stitches plus 3.
ROW 1 (RS) Ch 1, sc in 2nd ch from hook, sc in each ch across, turn.

ROW 2 Ch 1, sc in first sc, *ch 3, sk next sc, sc in next sc, ch 4, sk next 3 sc, bobble in next sc, ch 4, sk next 3 sc, sc in next sc; repeat from * across, ending with ch 3, sk next sc, sc in next sc. Fasten off.

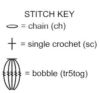

STITCH KEY
⌒ = chain (ch)
+ = single crochet (sc)
))))) = bobble (tr5tog)

Strikethrough Circles

Ch a multiple of 9 stitches plus 2.

ROUND 1 (RS) Sl st in 2nd ch from hook, sl st in next ch, *ch 10, sk next 6 ch**, sl st in next 3 ch; repeat from * across, ending last repeat at **, sl st in next ch, leaving last ch unworked; turn to work across opposite side of foundation ch; repeat from * across, ending last repeat at **, sl st in next ch, sl st in next ch, sl st in first sl st to join.

ROUND 2 *13 hdc in next ch-10 lp, sk next sl st, sl st in next sl st; repeat from * across, sl st in last unworked ch of foundation ch; repeat from * across opposite side of Round 1, sl st in first sl st to join. Fasten off.

STITCH KEY
- ⌒ = chain (ch)
- • = slip st (sl st)
- ⊤ = half double crochet (hdc)

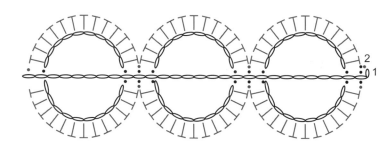

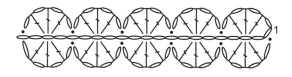

Pinwheels

Ch a multiple of 4 stitches plus 1.

ROUND 1 (RS) (Ch 1, dc) 3 times in 4th ch from hook, ch 1, sk next ch, sl st in next ch, *sk next ch, (ch 1, dc) 3 times in next ch, ch 1, sk next ch, sl st into next ch; repeat from * across to last ch, turn to work across opposite side of foundation chain; repeat from * across. Fasten off.

VARIATION: *Work only the top side of the foundation chain for a half-circle design.*

STITCH KEY
- ⌒ = chain (ch)
- • = slip st (sl st)
- ⊤ = double crochet (dc)

Shells

Picot Fans

PICOT Ch 3, sl st in 3rd ch from hook.

Ch a multiple of 12 stitches plus 1.
ROW 1 (RS) Ch 1, sc in 2nvd ch from hook, sc in each ch across, turn.
ROW 2 Ch 1, sc in first sc, *ch 5, sk next 3 sc, sc in next sc; repeat from * across, turn.
ROW 3 Ch 5 (counts as dc, ch 2), sc in next ch-5 sp, 8 dc in next ch-5 sp, sc in next ch-5 sp, *ch 5, sc in next ch-5 sp, 8 dc in next ch-5 sp, sc in next ch-5 sp; repeat from * across, ending with ch 2, dc in last sc, turn.
ROW 4 Ch 1, sc in first dc, sk next sc, *dc in next dc, (picot, dc) in each of next 7 dc, sc in next ch-5 sp, sk next sc; repeat from * across to turning ch, sk next 2 ch, sc in 3rd ch of turning ch. Fasten off.

STITCH KEY
⊖ = chain (ch)
• = slip st (sl st)
+ = single crochet (sc)
╦ = double crochet (dc)
◯•◯ = picot

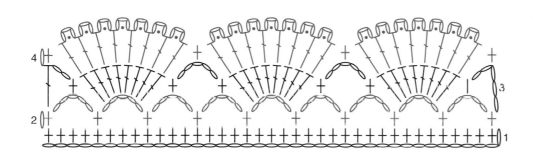

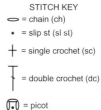

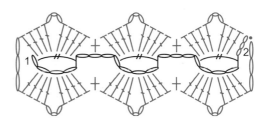

Diamonds

ROW 1 (RS) Ch 4, tr in 4th ch from hook, *ch 7, tr in 4th ch from hook; repeat from * until trim measures desired length.
ROUND 2 Working back across the tr edge of Row 1, ch 3 (counts as dc), (3 dc, ch 3, 4 dc) around the post of first tr, *sk next ch, sc in next ch, sk next ch, (4 dc, ch 3, 4 dc) around the post of next tr; repeat from * across, turn to work across opposite side of Row 1, (4 dc, ch 3, 4 dc) in first ch-3 lp; working in ch-3 lps, repeat from * across, ending with ch 3, sl st in top of beginning ch to join. Fasten off.

STITCH KEY
⊖ = chain (ch)
• = slip st (sl st)
+ = single crochet (sc)
╦ = double crochet (dc)
╪ = treble crochet (tr)

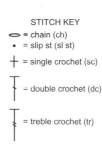

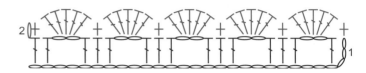

Arched Shells

Ch a multiple of 5 stitches.

ROW 1 (WS) Ch 3 (counts as dc), dc in 4th ch from hook, *ch 2, sk next 2 ch, dc in next 3 dc; repeat from * across, ending with dc in each of last 2 ch, turn.

ROW 2 (RS) Ch 1, sc in first dc, *sk next dc, 5 dc in next ch-2 sp, sk next dc, sc in next dc; repeat from * across, ending with last sc in top of turning ch. Fasten off.

STITCH KEY
⬭ = chain (ch)
+ = single crochet (sc)
T = double crochet (dc)

Mini Scallops

Ch a multiple of 2 stitches plus 1.

ROW 1 (WS) Ch 1, sc in 2nd ch from hook, sc in each ch across, turn.

ROW 2 (RS) Ch 1, sk first sc, *hdc in next sc, ch 1, sl st in next sc**, ch 1; repeat from * across, ending last repeat at **. Fasten off.

STITCH KEY
⬭ = chain (ch)
• = slip st (sl st)
+ = single crochet (sc)
T = half double crochet (hdc)

Floral Trims and Insertions

Petal Edge

Ch a multiple of 6 stitches plus 1.

ROW 1 (WS) Ch 1, sc in 2nd ch from hook, sc in each ch across, turn.

ROW 2 (RS) Sl st in first sc, *sk next 2 sc, (dc, ch 3, sl st, ch 3, dc, ch 3, sl st, ch 3, dc) in next sc, sk next 2 sc, sl st in next sc; repeat from * across. Fasten off.

STITCH KEY
◯ = chain (ch)
• = slip st (sl st)
+ = single crochet (sc)
⊤ = double crochet (dc)

 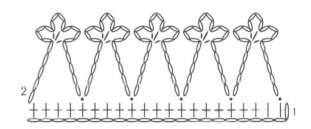

Picot Flowers

Ch a multiple of 4 stitches plus 1.

ROW 1 (WS) Ch 1, sc in 2nd ch from hook, sc in each ch across, turn.

ROW 2 (RS) *Ch 9, sl st in 5th ch from hook, (ch 4, sl st in same ch as last sl st) twice, ch 5, sk next 3 sc, sl st in next sc; repeat from * across. Fasten off.

STITCH KEY
◯ = chain (ch)
| or • = slip st (sl st)
+ = single crochet (sc)

Half Daisies

Ch a multiple of 11 stitches.

ROW 1 (WS) Ch 1, sc in 2nd ch from hook, sc in each ch across, turn.

ROW 2 (RS) Ch 3 (counts as hdc, ch 1), sk next sc, hdc in next sc, *ch 1, sk next sc, hdc in next sc; repeat from * across, turn.

ROW 3 Ch 1, *sc in next 4 stitches, ch 6, sk next 3 stitches, sc in next 4 stitches; repeat from * across, turn.

ROW 4 Sl st in first stitch, *(tr, ch 4, sl st, [ch 4, tr, ch 4, sl st] twice, ch 4, tr) in next ch-6 lp, sk next 3 sc, sl st in each of next 2 sc; repeat from * across, ending with sl st in last sc. Fasten off.

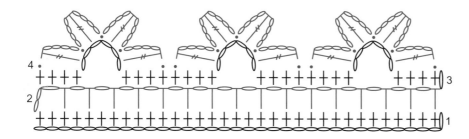

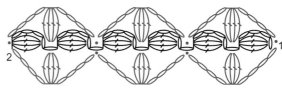

Floral Diamonds

DOUBLE CROCHET 4 TOGETHER CLUSTER (dc4tog) (Yo, insert hook in stitch, yo, draw yarn through stitch, yo, draw yarn through 2 lps on hook) 4 times in same stitch, yo, draw yarn through 5 lps on hook.

ROW 1 (RS) Ch 4, dc4tog in 4th ch from hook, *ch 5, dc4tog in 4th ch from hook; repeat from * until trim measures desired length; the number of dc4tog clusters should be a multiple of 2.

ROUND 2 Working back across Row 1, *ch 4, sk next cluster, dc4tog in ch between 2 clusters, ch 4, sk next cluster, sl st in next ch between 2 clusters; repeat from * across, ending with sl st in ch at base of last cluster, turn to work across bottom side of Row 1, repeat from * across, ending with a sl st in top of last cluster. Fasten off.

Looped Petals

TREBLE 2 TOGETHER CLUSTER (tr2tog) (Yo twice, insert hook in stitch, yo, draw yarn through stitch, [yo, draw yarn through 2 lps on hook] twice) 2 times in same stitch, yo, draw yarn through 3 lps on hook.

TREBLE 3 TOGETHER CLUSTER (tr3tog) (Yo twice, insert hook in stitch, yo, draw yarn through stitch, [yo, draw yarn through 2 lps on hook] twice) 3 times in same stitch, yo, draw yarn through 4 lps on hook.

TREBLE 6 TOGETHER CLUSTER (tr6tog) *(Yo twice, insert hook in ch-10 lp, yo, draw yarn through stitch, [yo, draw yarn through 2 lps on hook] twice) 3 times in first ch-10 lp; repeat from * in next ch-10 lp, yo, draw yarn through 7 lps on hook.

ROW 1 (WS) *Ch 10, tr3tog in 10th ch from hook**, ch 4, tr2tog in 4th ch from hook; repeat from * until trim measures desired length, ending last repeat at **, turn.

ROW 2 (RS) Sl st in first ch of ch-9 lp, ch 4, (tr3tog, ch 5) twice in next ch-9 lp, *work tr6tog (working 3 tr in same ch-9 lp and 3 tr in next ch-9 lp), ch 5, tr3tog in same ch-9 lp**, ch 5; repeat from * across, ending last repeat at **, ch 4, sl st in ch at base of last cluster. Fasten off.

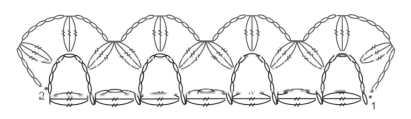

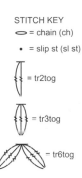

STITCH KEY
- ⬭ = chain (ch)
- • = slip st (sl st)
- ⫝̸ = tr2tog
- ⫝̸ = tr3tog
- ⟋⟍ = tr6tog

Vintage Inspired

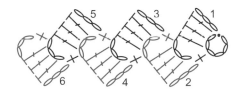

Rick-Rack

Ch 6, join with a sl st to form a ring.
ROW 1 (RS) (Ch 3, 3 dc, ch 3, sc) into ring, turn.
ROW 2 (Ch 3, 3 dc, ch 3, sc) into next ch-3 sp, turn.

Repeat Row 2 until trim measures desired length. Fasten off.

STITCH KEY
- ⬭ = chain (ch)
- • = slip st (sl st)
- + = single crochet (sc)
- ⊤ = double crochet (dc)

 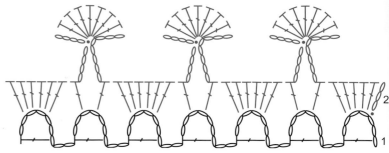

Pom-Poms

ROW 1 (RS) Ch 7, dc in 7th ch from hook, *ch 9, dc in 7th ch from hook; repeat from * until work measures slightly longer than desired length. Fasten off.

ROW 2 With right side facing, join yarn in first ch-6 lp, ch 3 (counts as dc), 5 dc in same lp, *dc in next ch-6 lp, ch 8, (7 dc, ch 4, sl st) in 4th ch from hook, ch 4, dc in same ch-6 lp in Row 1, 6 dc in next ch-6 lp; repeat from * across. Fasten off.

STITCH KEY
⬯ = chain (ch)
• = slip st (sl st)
T = double crochet (dc)

Triangles

Ch a multiple of 4 stitches plus 1.

ROW 1 (RS) Work 3 dc in 5th ch from hook, *sk next 3 ch, (sc, ch 3, 3 dc) in next ch; repeat from * across. Fasten off.

STITCH KEY
⬯ = chain (ch)
+ = single crochet (sc)
T = double crochet (dc)

 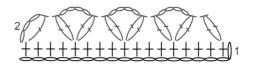

Looped Xs

DOUBLE CROCHET 2 TOGETHER CLUSTER (dc2tog) (Yo, insert hook in stitch, yo, draw yarn through stitch, yo, draw yarn through 2 lps on hook) twice in same stitch, yo, draw yarn through 3 lps on hook.

Ch a multiple of 4 stitches plus 1.

ROW 1 (WS) Ch 1, sc in 2nd ch from hook, sc in each ch across, turn.

ROW 2 (RS) Ch 3, dc in first sc (counts as dc2tog), *sk next 3 sc, (dc2tog, ch 4, dc2tog) in next sc; repeat from * across to within last 4 sc, sk next 3 sc, dc2tog in last sc. Fasten off.

STITCH KEY
⬯ = chain (ch)
+ = single crochet (sc)
T = double crochet (dc)
⋔ = dc2tog

Add-ons and Embellishments

Beads

NOTE: *Thread all beads onto the yarn before crocheting. You will need three seed beads per beaded stitch.*

BEADED DOUBLE CROCHET (bdc) Yo, insert hook in stitch, yo, draw up lp, yo, draw through 2 lps on hook, bring 3 beads to working yarn and let them fall to the back of the stitch, yo, draw through remaining 2 lps on hook.

Ch a multiple of 2 stitches plus 1.
ROW 1 (WS) Ch 1, sc in 2nd ch from hook, sc in each ch across, turn.

ROW 2 (RS) Ch 3 (counts as dc), *BDC in next sc, dc in next dc; repeat from * across, turn.

ROW 3 (WS) Ch 1, sc in each stitch across, turn.

ROW 4 (WS) Ch 1, sc in first sc, *ch 3, sk next sc, sc in next sc; repeat from * across. Fasten off.

ROW 5 (RS) With right side facing, join yarn in first ch on opposite side of foundation ch, ch 1, sc in first ch, *ch 3, sk next ch, sc in next ch; repeat from * across. Fasten off.

STITCH KEY
⬭ = chain (ch)
✛ = single crochet (sc)
┬ = double crochet (dc)
⫯ = beaded double crochet (BDC)

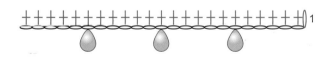

Briolettes

NOTE: *Thread all beads onto the yarn before crocheting. You will need one bead for every 6 stitches of trim.*

FOUNDATION ROW *Ch 5, pull up a bead, (let bead fall to back of the stitch), ch 1; repeat from * across until trim is just shorter than desired length, ch 5.

ROW 1 (RS) Ch 1, sc in 2nd ch from hook, sc in each ch across. Fasten off.

STITCH KEY
⬭ = chain (ch)
◗ = beaded ch
✛ = single crochet (sc)

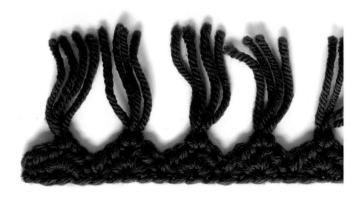

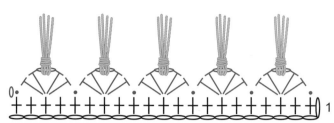

Fringe

Ch a multiple of 4 stitches plus 1.

ROW 1 (WS) Ch 1, sc in 2nd ch from hook, sc in each ch across, turn.

ROW 2 (RS) Ch 1, sl st in first sc, *sk next sc, (2 hdc, ch 1, 2 hdc) in next sc, sk next sc, sl st in next sc; repeat from * across. Fasten off.

TO MAKE FRINGE IN EACH CH-1 SP Cut two 6" (15cm) strands of yarn, hold them together, and fold them in half to form a loop. With wrong side of trim facing, insert hook in ch-1 sp, pull loop end of yarn strands through sp, wrap four yarn ends around hook, pull through loop, and pull ends taut. Once all fringe has been attached, trim the strands to an equal length.

STITCH KEY

⌒ = chain (ch)

• = slip st (sl st)

+ = single crochet (sc)

T = half double crochet (hdc)

= fringe

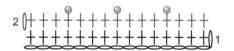

Sequins

NOTE: *Thread all sequins onto the yarn before crocheting. You will need one sequin for every 4 stitches of trim.*

SEQUIN SINGLE CROCHET (ssc) Insert hook in stitch, yo, draw yarn through stitch, bring sequin up to hook (let it fall to back of stitch), yo, draw yarn through both loops to complete sc.

Ch a multiple of 4 stitches plus 3.

ROW 1 (RS) Ch 1, working in bottom lps of foundation ch, sc in 2nd ch from hook, sc in each ch across, turn.

ROW 2 (WS) Ch 1, sc in first 3 sc, *SSC in next st, sc in each of next 3 sc; repeat from * across. Fasten off.

STITCH KEY

⌒ = chain (ch)

+ = single crochet (sc)

= sequin single crochet (SSC)

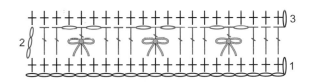

Bows

Ch a multiple of 6 stitches plus 3.
ROW 1 (RS) Ch 1, sc in 2nd ch from hook, sc in each ch across, turn.
ROW 2 (WS) Ch 3 (counts as dc), dc in next 2 dc, *(ch 1, sk next sc, dc in next sc) twice, dc in next 2 dc; repeat from * across, turn.
ROW 3 (RS) Ch 1, sc in each stitch and sp across. Fasten off.

TYING BOWS Cut a 5" (12.5cm) length of contrasting yarn and thread it in and out of one pair of ch-1 sps with right side of trim facing you. Tie ends in a bow. Repeat as many times as necessary and trim bow ends to a consistent length.

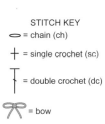

STITCH KEY
⬯ = chain (ch)
✛ = single crochet (sc)
† = double crochet (dc)
🎀 = bow

Woven Ribbon

Ch a multiple of 7 stitches plus 2.
ROW 1 (RS) Ch 1, sc in 2nd ch from hook, sc in each ch across, turn.
ROW 2 (WS) Ch 3 (counts as dc), dc in next sc, *(ch 3, sk next 2 sc, dc in next dc) twice, dc in next dc; repeat from * across, turn.
ROW 3 (RS) Sl st in first 2 dc, *(4 hdc in next ch-2 sp, sl st in dc) twice, sl st in next dc; repeat from * across. Fasten off.

With right side of trim facing you, insert ribbon from back to front in first sp created by ch-2, weave over dc, under 2 dc, over dc, under 2 dc and so on. Tie ends in a bow or stitch to back of trim to secure and conceal.

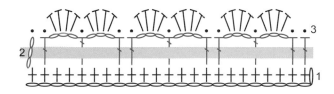

STITCH KEY
⬯ = chain (ch)
• = slip st (sl st)
✛ = single crochet (sc)
† = half double crochet (hdc)
† = double crochet (dc)
▭ = ribbon

Motifs

Crochet motifs come in all shapes and sizes, from flowers and natural silhouettes to medallions and geometric shapes. Experiment with ways to use these motifs throughout your wardrobe.

Here are some creative ways to make them yours:

- Play with gauge—the thicker the yarn, the bigger the motif.

- Try changing colors at the end of every round, or use a variegated yarn for a multicolored effect.

- Use novelty yarns to add texture to your motifs.

- Crochet motifs with 100 percent wool yarn, then felt them for fuzzy fun. To felt motifs, place them in a mesh bag and run them through your washer on the hot wash/cold rinse cycle. Lay them flat to dry, or shrink them further by running them through the dryer.

- Combine your favorite elements from several motifs to make your own shapes!

- Remember that you can also use the medallions, flowers, and natural shapes from the projects in this book as motifs to make something entirely different. For instance, work the Leaf from the Leaf Earrings (page 82) in worsted weight yarn to embellish a tote, or try making the medallions from the Medallion Table Mat (page 102) in crochet thread and scatter them on a sweater.

Flowers

STITCH KEY
⬭ = chain (ch)
• = slip st (sl st)
+ = single crochet (sc)
↘ = placement of stitch

Loopy Flower

Ch 6, join with a sl st to form a ring.
ROUND 1 (RS) Ch 1, 10 sc in ring, sl st in first sc to join—10 sc.
ROUND 2 Ch 1, sc in first sc, *ch 10, sc in next sc; repeat from * around, ending with ch 10, sl st to first sc to join—10 ch-10 lps.

ROUND 3 Working behind previous round of petals, *ch 12, sk next ch-10 lp, sc in next sc from Round 1 (already holding a sc); repeat from * around, sc in last sc to join—10 ch-12 lps.

ROUND 4 Working behind previous round of petals, *ch 15, sk next ch-12 petal, sc in next sc in Round 3; repeat from * around, sl st in first ch to join—10 ch-15 lps.
Fasten off.

Pinwheel Posy

Ch 8, join with a sl st to form a ring.

ROUND 1 (RS) Ch 1, 15 sc in ring, sl st in first sc to join—15 sc.

ROUND 2 Ch 5 (counts as dc, ch 2), (dc, ch 2) in each sc around, sl st in 3rd ch of beginning ch to join—15 ch-2 sps.

ROUND 3 Ch 1, sc in first stitch, 2 sc in next ch-2 sp, *sc in next dc, 2 sc in next ch-2 sp; repeat from * around, join—45 sc.

ROUND 4 Ch 1, *sc in next sc, ch 10, sl st in first ch to form lp, sc in each of next 2 sc; repeat from * around, join—15 ch-10 lps.

ROUND 5 *(Sc, hdc, 10 dc, hdc, sc) in next ch-10 lp, sl st in each of next 3 sc; repeat from * around, join—15 petals. Fasten off.

STITCH KEY
⬯ = chain (ch)
• = slip st (sl st)
+ = single crochet (sc)
T = half double crochet (hdc)
┬ = double crochet (dc)

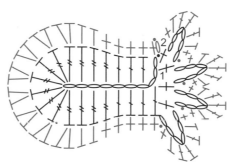

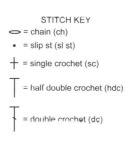

STITCH KEY
⬯ = chain (ch)
• = slip st (sl st)
+ = single crochet (sc)
T = half double crochet (hdc)
┬ = double crochet (dc)
╪ = treble crochet (tr)

Blooming Bud

Ch 10.

ROUND 1 (RS) Dc in 4th ch from hook (counts as first 2 dc), dc in each of next 2 ch, tr in each of next 3 ch, 8 tr in last ch, turning to work across opposite side of foundation ch, tr in each of next 3 ch, dc in each of next 4 ch, *ch 6, sc in side of dc on short edge; working across edge of piece, repeat from * 2 times more, ch 6, sl st in top of beginning ch to join.

ROUND 2 Ch 1, sc in first stitch, sc in each of next 4 stitches, hdc in each of next 2 stitches, 2 hdc in each of next 8 stitches, hdc in each of next 2 stitches, sc in each of next 5 stitches, (sl st, sc, hdc, 3 dc, hdc, sc) in each of next 4 ch-6 lps, sl st in first sc to join—58 stitches. Fasten off.

Flowers

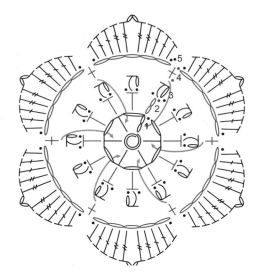

Daffodil

With first color, make a magic ring.

ROUND 1 (RS) Ch 3 (counts as hdc, ch 1), (hdc, ch 1) into ring 5 times, sl st to 2nd ch of beginning ch to join—6 ch-1 sps.

ROUND 2 Ch 2, hdc in first ch-1 sp, 2 hdc in each remaining ch-1 sp of round, sl st in top of beginning ch to join—12 hdc.

ROUND 3 Ch 1, (hdc, sl st) in first hdc, *(sl st, ch 1, hdc, sl st) in next hdc; repeat from * around—12 hdc. Fasten off first color.

ROUND 4 Working behind stitches in last 2 rounds, join 2nd color around the beginning ch in Round 1, sc around the post of same hdc, ch 5, *sc around the post of next hdc in Round 1, ch 5; repeat from * around, sl st in first sc to join—6 ch-5 lps.

ROUND 5 Work (sl st, hdc, 2 dc, 2 tr, ch 2, 2 tr, 2 dc, hdc, sl st) in each ch-5 lp around, sl st in first sl st to join—6 petals. Fasten off.

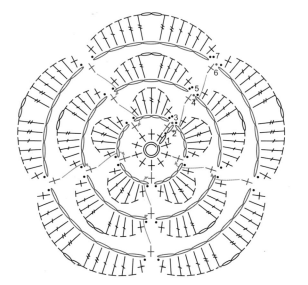

Buttercup

With first color, make a magic ring.

ROUND 1 (RS) Ch 1, 10 sc in ring, sl st in first sc to join—10 sc.

ROUND 2 Ch 1, *sc in sc, ch 4, sk next sc; repeat from * 4 times more, sl st in first sc to join—5 ch-4 lps.

ROUND 3 Work (sl st, sc, hdc, dc, tr, dc, hdc, sc, sl st) in each ch-4 lp around, sl st in first sl st to join —5 petals. Fasten off first color.

ROUND 4 Working behind petals in Round 3, join 2nd color around the post of the first sc in Round 2, sc around the post of same sc, ch 5, *sc around the post of next sc in Round 2, ch 5; repeat from * around, sl st in first sc to join—5 ch-5 lps.

ROUND 5 Work (sl st, sc, hdc, 2 dc, tr, ch 2, tr, 2 dc, hdc, sc, sl st) in each ch-5 lp around, sl st in first sl st to join—5 petals. Fasten off 2nd color.

ROUND 6 Working behind petals in Round 5, join 3rd color around the post of the first sc in Round 4 sc around the post of same sc, ch 7, *sc around the post of next sc in Round 4, ch 7; repeat from * around, sl st in first sc to join—5 ch-7 lps.

ROUND 7 Work (sl st, sc, hdc, 3 dc, 2 tr, ch 2, 2 tr, 3 dc, hdc, sc, sl st) in each ch-7 lp around, sl st to first sl st to join—5 petals. Fasten off.

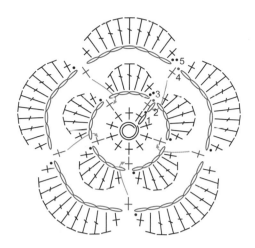

Rose

Make a magic ring.

ROUND 1 (RS) Ch 1, 10 sc in ring, sl st in first sc to join—10 sc.

ROUND 2 Ch 1, sc in first sc, *ch 4, sk next sc, sc in next sc; repeat from * 3 times more, ending with ch 4, sk next sc, sl st in first sc of round to join—5 ch-4 lps.

ROUND 3 Sl st in first ch-4 lp, *(sc, hdc, 3 dc, hdc, sc) in ch-4 lp, sl st in next ch-4 lp; repeat from * around, sl st in first sl st to join—5 petals.

ROUND 4 Working behind petals in Round 3, ch 1, sc around the post of first sc in Round 2, ch 7, sk next petal, *sc around the post of next sc from Round 2, ch 7, sk next petal; repeat from * around, sl st to first sc of round to join—5 ch-7 lps.

ROUND 5 Work (sl st, sc, hdc, 7 dc, hdc, sc) in each ch-7 lp around, sl st in first sl st to join—5 petals. Fasten off.

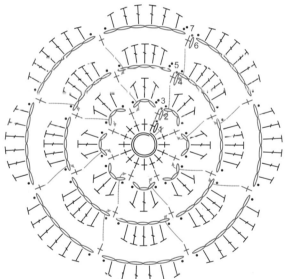

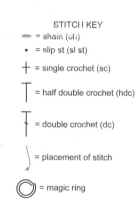

Ranunculus

Make a magic ring.

ROUND 1 (RS) Ch 1, 16 sc in ring, sl st in first sc to join—16 sc.

ROUND 2 Ch 1, sc in first sc, ch 3, sk next sc, *sc in next sc, ch 3, sk next sc; repeat from * around, sl st in first sc to join—8 ch-3 lps.

ROUND 3 (Sl st, hdc, dc, hdc, sl st) in each ch-3 lp around, sl st in first sl st to join—8 petals.

ROUND 4 Ch 1, working behind petals in Round 3, sc around the post of first sc in Round 2, ch 5, sk next petal, *sc around the post of next sc in Round 2, ch 5, sk next petal; repeat from * around, sl st to first sc to join—8 ch-5 lps.

ROUND 5 (Sl st, hdc, 3 dc, hdc, sl st) in each ch-5 lp around, sl st in first sl st to join—8 petals.

ROUND 6 Ch 1, working behind petals in Round 5, sc around the post of first sc in Round 4, ch 6, sk next petal, *sc around the post of next sc in Round 4, ch 6, sk next petal; repeat from * around, sl st in first sc to join—8 ch-6 lps.

ROUND 7 Work (sl st, hdc, 4 dc, hdc, sl st) in each ch-6 lp around, sl st in first sl st to join—8 petals. Fasten off.

Geometric Shapes

Mitered Square

NOTE: *This square is made by adding a (sc, ch 2, sc) increase to the center ch-2 of each row.*

Make a magic ring.

ROW 1 (RS) With first color, ch 1, 3 sc in ring, turn—3 sc.

ROW 2 (WS) Ch 1, sc in next sc, (sc, ch 2, sc) in next sc, sc in last sc, turn—4 sc.

ROW 3 (RS) Ch 1, sc in next 2 sc, (sc, ch 2, sc) in ch-2 sp, sc in last 2 sc, turn—6 sc.

ROW 4 (WS) Ch 1, sc in next 3 sc, (sc, ch 2, sc) in ch-2 sp, sc in last 3 sc, turn—8 sc. Fasten off first color. With right side facing, join 2nd color in first sc.

ROW 5 (RS) Ch 1, sc in each sc to next corner ch-2 sp, (sc, ch 2, sc) in ch-2 sp, sc in each remaining sc, turn—10 sc.

ROWS 6–10 With right side facing, join 2nd color. Repeat Row 5. At end of Row 10, fasten off 2nd color.

ROWS 11–18 With right side facing, join 3rd color in first sc. Repeat Row 5. Fasten off.

VARIATION: *Change colors as desired, working as many rows as desired. This pattern is also great for variegated yarns.*

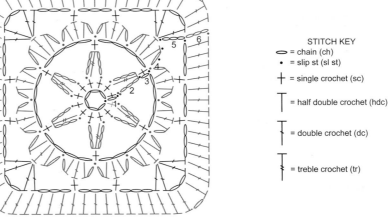

Framed Flower

With first color, ch 6, join with a sl st to form a ring.

ROUND 1 (RS) Ch 1, 12 sc in ring, sl st in first sc to join—12 sc. Fasten off first color.

ROUND 2 With right side facing, join 2nd color in first sc in Round 1, ch 3, (tr, ch 3, sl st) in next sc, *sl st in next sc, ch 3, (tr, ch 3, sl st) in next sc; repeat from * 4 times more, sl st in first stitch to join—6 petals. Fasten off 2nd color.

ROUND 3 With right side facing, join first color in first tr of Round 2, ch 1, sc in tr, *ch 4, sc in tr of next petal; repeat from * around, ending with ch 4, sl st in first sc to join—6 ch-4 lps.

ROUND 4 *(Ch 1, hdc, dc, hdc, ch 1, sl st, ch 1, hdc, dc, hdc, ch 1) in next ch-4 lp, sl st in next sc; repeat from * around, sl st in first sl st to join—12 petals.

ROUND 5 Sl st to next dc, ch 3 (counts as dc), (dc, ch 2, 2 dc) in first dc, *(ch 3, sc in center dc of next petal) twice, ch 3**, (2 dc, ch 3, 2 dc) in next dc; repeat from * around, ending last repeat at **, sl st in top of beginning ch to join—12 ch-3 sps; 4 ch-2 corners.

ROUND 6 Ch 3 (counts as dc), dc in each of next 2 stitches, ch 1 (corner), *dc in each of next 17 stitches, ch 1; repeat from * two times, dc in each remaining stitch of round, sl st in top of beginning ch to join—68 dc; 4 ch-1 sps. Fasten off.

Spanish Tile Square

DOUBLE CROCHET 2 TOGETHER CLUSTER (dc2tog) (Yo, insert hook in next stitch, yo, draw yarn through stitch, yo, draw yarn through 2 lps on hook) twice in same stitch, yo, draw yarn through 3 lps on hook.

DOUBLE CROCHET 3 TOGETHER CLUSTER (dc3tog) (Yo, insert hook in stitch, yo, draw yarn through stitch, yo, draw yarn through 2 lps on hook) 3 times in same stitch, yo, draw yarn through 4 lps on hook.

Make a magic ring.

ROUND 1 (RS) With first color, ch 3, dc2tog (counts as dc3tog) in ring, ch 4, (dc3tog in ring, ch 4) 3 times, sl st in first cluster to join—4 clusters.

ROUND 2 With right side facing, join 2nd color in first cluster in Round 1, ch 1, *sc in cluster, 7 dc in next ch-4 sp; repeat from * around, sl st in first sc to join—4 petals. Fasten off 2nd color.

ROUND 3 With first color, ch 3, dc in first sc (counts as first dc2tog), *ch 3, sk next 3 dc, sc in next dc, ch 3, sk next 3 dc, (dc2tog,

ch 5, dc2tog) in next sc; repeat from * twice more, ch 3, sk next 3 dc, sc in next dc, ch 3, dc2tog in sc, ch 5, sl st in first dc to join—8 ch-3 sps; 4 ch-5 corner sps. Fasten off first color.

ROUND 4 With right side facing, join 3rd color in ch-3 sp to the left of any corner ch-5 sp, ch 3 (counts as dc), 2 dc in first ch-3 sp, ch 1, *3 dc in next ch-3 sp, ch 1, (3 dc, ch 3, 3 dc) in next corner ch-5 sp, ch 1**, 3 dc in next ch-3 sp, ch 1*; repeat from * to * twice more, repeat from * to ** once more, sl st in top of beginning ch to join—12 ch-1 sps; 4 ch-3 sps. Fasten off.

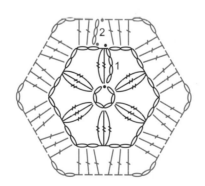

Flower Hexagon

TREBLE 2 TOGETHER CLUSTER (tr2tog) (Yo twice, insert hook in stitch, yo, draw yarn through stitch, [yo, draw yarn through 2 lps on hook] twice) twice in same stitch, yo, draw yarn through 3 lps on hook.

TREBLE 3 TOGETHER CLUSTER (tr3tog) (Yo twice, insert hook in stitch, yo, draw yarn through stitch, [yo, draw yarn through 2 lps on hook] twice) 3 times in same stitch, yo, draw yarn through 4 lps on hook.

Ch 6, join with a sl st to form ring.

ROUND 1 (RS) Ch 4, tr2tog in ring (counts as tr3tog), ch 4, (tr3tog, ch 4) 5 times in ring, sl st in top of first cluster to join—6 petals.

ROUND 2 Sl st in next ch, ch 3 (counts as dc), (2 dc, ch 3, 3 dc) in first ch-4 sp, (3 dc, ch 3, 3dc) in each ch-4 sp around, sl st in top of beginning ch to join—36 dc; 6 ch-3 corner sps. Fasten off.

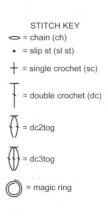

Hexagons

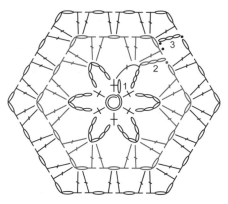

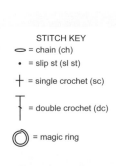

STITCH KEY

⬯ = chain (ch)

• = slip st (sl st)

✛ = single crochet (sc)

⊥ = double crochet (dc)

◎ = magic ring

Loopy Flower Hexagon

Make a magic ring.

ROUND 1 (RS) Ch 1, (sc, ch 6) 5 times in ring, ch 3, dc in first sc to join—6 ch-6 lps.

ROUND 2 Ch 3 (counts as dc here and throughout), (dc, ch 2, 2 dc) in first lp,

ch 1, *(2 dc, ch 2, 2 dc) in next ch-6 lp, ch 1; repeat from * around, sl st in top of beginning ch to join—24 dc; 6 ch-2 corner sps.

ROUND 3 Sl st to first ch-2 sp, ch 3, (dc, ch

2, 2 dc) in first ch-2 sp, *ch 1, 2 dc in next ch-1 sp, ch 1, (2 dc, ch 2, 2dc) in next ch-3 sp; repeat from * 4 times more, ch 1, 2 dc in next ch-1 sp, ch 1, sl st in top of beginning ch to join—36 dc; 6 ch-2 corner sps. Fasten off.

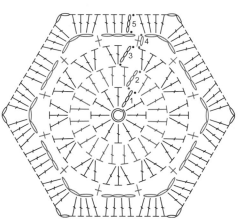

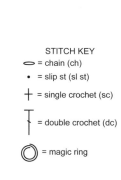

STITCH KEY

⬯ = chain (ch)

• = slip st (sl st)

✛ = single crochet (sc)

⊥ = double crochet (dc)

◎ = magic ring

Granny Hexagon

NOTE: *To achieve the puffed look of this hexagon, make your stitches into the space between stitches (not under the V).*

With first color, make a magic ring.

ROUND 1 (RS) Ch 3 (counts as first dc here and throughout), 11 dc in ring, sl st in top of beginning ch to join—12 dc.

ROUND 2 With right side facing, join 2nd color in sp between first 2 stitches of

previous round, ch 3, dc in same sp, 2 dc in sp between each dc around, sl st in top of beginning ch to join—24 dc.

ROUND 3 With right side facing, join 3rd color in sp between first two 2-dc sets, ch 3, 2 dc in same sp, 3 dc in each remaining sp between 2-dc sets of previous round, sl st in top of beginning ch to join—36 dc.

ROUND 4 With right side facing, join 4th color in sp between first two 3-dc sets of previous round, ch 1, sc in same sp, ch 3, *sk

next 3 dc, sc in sp between two 3-dc sets, ch 3; repeat from * around, sl st in first sc to join—12 ch-3 sps.

ROUND 5 Sl st in first ch-3 sp, ch 3, 3 dc in first ch-3 sp, *(4 dc, ch 2, 4 dc) in next ch-3 sp, 4 dc in next ch-3 sp; repeat from * 4 times, (4 dc, ch 2, 4 dc) in last ch-3 sp, sl st in top of beginning ch to join—72 dc, 6 ch-2 corner sps. Fasten off.

Triangles

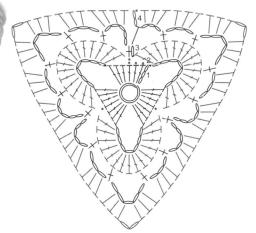

Triple Loop Triangle

Make a magic ring.

ROUND 1 (RS) Ch 3 (counts as dc), 6 dc in ring, ch 7, (7 dc in ring, ch 7) twice, sl st in top of beginning ch to join—21 dc; 3 ch-7 lps.

ROUND 2 Sl st in next 3 dc, (15 dc in next ch-7 lp, sk next 3 dc, sl st in next dc) 3 times, sl st in 3rd sl st of round to join—45 dc.

ROUND 3 Ch 1, sc in first stitch, *(ch 5, sk next 2 dc, sc in next dc, ch 3, sk next 2 dc, sc in next dc) twice, ch 5, sk 2 dc, sc in next dc; repeat from * twice more, omitting last (ch 5, sc), ending with ch-3, hdc in first sc instead of last ch-5 lp—9 ch-5 lps; 6 ch-3 lps.

ROUND 4 Ch 2 (counts as hdc), *4 hdc in next ch-5 lp, 3 hdc in next ch-3 lp, (3 hdc, ch 2, 3 hdc) in next ch-5 lp, 3 hdc in next ch-3 lp, 4 hdc in next ch-5 lp; repeat from * twice more, ending with 3 hdc in last ch-5 lp, sl st in top of beginning ch to join—60 hdc. Fasten off.

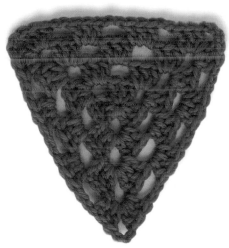

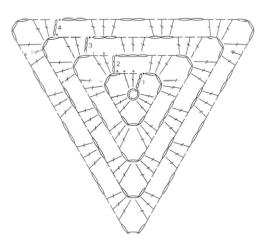

Granny Triangle

Make a magic ring.

ROUND 1 (RS) Ch 3 (counts as dc here and throughout), 2 dc in ring, (ch 3, 3 dc in ring) twice, ch 3, sl st in top of beginning ch to join—9 dc; 3 ch-3 sps.

ROUND 2 Sl st in next 3 stitches, ch 3, (2 dc, ch 3, 3 dc) in first ch-3 sp, *ch 3, sk next 3 dc, (3 dc, ch 3, 3 dc) in next ch-3 sp;

repeat from * once more, ch 3, sl st in top of beginning ch to join—18 dc; 6 ch-3 sps.

ROUND 3 Sl st in next 3 stitches, ch 3, (2 dc, ch 3, 3 dc) in first ch-3 sp, *ch 2, sk next 3 dc, 3 dc in next ch-1 sp, ch 2, sk next 3 dc, (3 dc, ch 3, 3 dc) in next ch-3 sp; repeat from * once more, 3 dc in next ch-3 sp, ch 2, sl st in top of beginning ch to join—27 dc; 3 ch-3 sps; 6 ch-2 sps.

ROUND 4 Sl st in next 3 stitches, ch 3, (2 dc, ch 3, 3 dc) in first ch-3 sp, *ch 2, sk next 3 dc, (3 dc in next ch-2 sp, ch 2, sk next 3 dc) twice, sk next 3 dc, (3 dc, ch 3, 3 dc) in next ch-3 sp; repeat from * once more, (3 dc in next ch-2 sp, ch 2, sk next 3 dc) twice, sl st to top of beginning ch to join—27 dc; 3 ch-3 sps; 9 ch-2 sps. Fasten off.

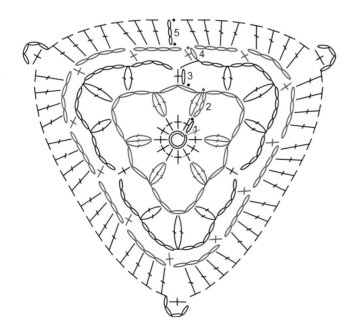

Flower Triangle

DOUBLE CROCHET 2 TOGETHER CLUSTER (dc2tog) (Yo, insert hook in stitch, yo, draw yarn through stitch, yo, draw yarn through 2 lps on hook) twice in same stitch, yo, draw yarn through 3 lps on hook.

DOUBLE CROCHET 3 TOGETHER CLUSTER (dc3tog) (Yo, insert hook in stitch, yo, draw yarn through stitch, yo, draw yarn through 2 lps on hook) 3 times in same stitch, yo, draw yarn through 4 lps on hook.

Make a magic ring.

ROUND 1 (RS) With first color, ch 1, 12 sc in ring, sl st in first sc to join—12 sc. Fasten off first color.

ROUND 2 With right side facing, join 2nd color in first sc in Round 1, ch 3, dc2tog in first sc (counts as dc3tog), *ch 2, sk next sc, dc3tog in next sc, ch 5,** sk next sc, dc3tog in next sc*; repeat from * to * once, repeat from * to ** once, sl st in first cluster to join—6 clusters. Fasten off 2nd color.

ROUND 3 With right side facing, join first color in any ch-2 sp, ch 1, sc in same ch-2 sp, *ch 4, (dc2tog, ch 4) three times in next ch-5 sp, ch 4, sc in next ch-2 sp; repeat from * twice more, omitting last (ch 4, sc), ending with ch 2, hdc in first sc of round to join (counts as last ch-4)—9 dc2tog; 12 ch-4 lps.

ROUND 4 Ch 1, (sc, ch 4) in each ch-4 lp around, sl st in first sc to join—12 ch-4 lps.

ROUND 5 Sl st in first ch-4 lp, ch 3, 3 dc in same ch-4 lp, *4 dc in next ch-4 lp, ch 4, sc in 4th ch from hook for picot, 4 dc in each of next 3 ch-4 lps; repeat from * once more, 4 dc in next ch-4 lp, ch 4, sc in 4th ch from hook for picot, 4 dc in each of next 2 ch-4 lps, sl st in top of beginning ch to join—48 dc; 3 picots. Fasten off.

Stitch Patterns

If you're seeking the perfect base for your next embellishment project, browse these stitch patterns and pick a favorite. You can use them to make anything from a scarf or bag to a skirt or sweater. I've included some classics and old favorites and devised a few new tricks, too. The stitch patterns are divided into sections based on the way they look, but all of the patterns are created by combining the basic stitches introduced in this book, so I encourage you to try something new.

You may find the textures of these stitch patterns so pleasing that your project needs no embellishment, but there are plenty of trims and motifs to choose from if you wish to make your piece extra special. Experiment with different yarn weights and textures for an array of surprising looks.

Basic Stitches and Combinations

Single Crochet
Ch any number of stitches.
ROW 1 (RS) Ch 1, sc in 2nd ch from hook, sc in each ch across, turn.
ROW 2 Ch 1, sc in each sc across, turn.

Repeat Row 2.

STITCH KEY
⌣ = chain (ch)

+ = single crochet (sc)

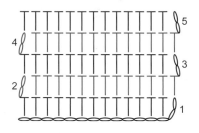

Half Double Crochet

Ch any number of stitches.

ROW 1 (RS) Ch 2 (counts as hdc throughout), hdc in 3rd ch from hook, hdc in each ch across, turn.

ROW 2 Ch 2, sk first hdc, hdc in each hdc across, turn.

Repeat Row 2.

STITCH KEY
⬭ = chain (ch)
T = half double crochet (hdc)

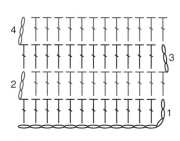

Double Crochet

Ch any number of stitches.

ROW 1 (RS) Ch 3 (counts as dc throughout), dc in 4th ch from hook, dc in each ch across, turn.

ROW 2 Ch 3, sk first dc, dc in each dc across, turn.

Repeat Row 2.

STITCH KEY
⬭ = chain (ch)
† = double crochet (dc)

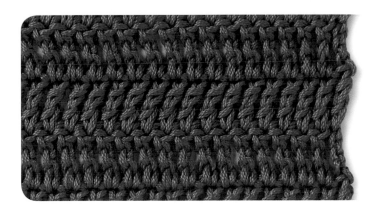

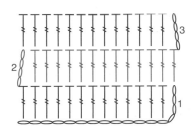

Treble Crochet

Ch any number of stitches.

ROW 1 (RS) Ch 4 (counts as tr throughout), tr in 5th ch from hook, tr in each ch across, turn.

ROW 2 Ch 4, sk first tr, tr in each tr across, turn.

Repeat Row 2.

STITCH KEY

◯ = chain (ch)

⊥ = treble crochet (tr)

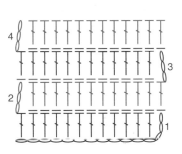

Faux Rib: Back Loop (BL) Double Crochet

Ch any number of stitches.

ROW 1 (RS) Ch 3 (counts as dc throughout), dc in 4th ch from hook, dc in each ch across, turn.

ROW 2 Ch 3, sk first dc, dc in BL of each dc across, turn.

Repeat Row 2.

VARIATIONS: *Try this with sc, hdc, and tr stitches.*

STITCH KEY

◯ = chain (ch)

| = double crochet (dc)

— = worked in back loop only

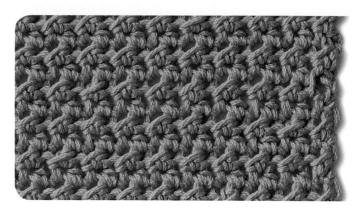

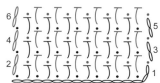

Combination Crunch (Half Double Crochet and Slip Stitch)

Ch a multiple of 2 stitches plus 1.

ROW 1 (RS) Ch 2 (counts as hdc throughout), sl st in 3rd ch from hook, *hdc in next ch, sl st in next ch; repeat from * across, turn.

ROW 2 Ch 2 (counts as hdc), sl st in next hdc, *hdc in next sc, sl st in next hdc; repeat from * across, turn.

Repeat Row 2.

VARIATIONS: *Replace hdc stitches with sc, dc, or tr stitches using the appropriate number of turning chains for each stitch at the beginning of each row.*

Textured Stitches

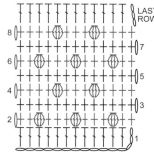

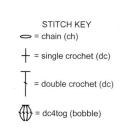

Bobble

NOTE: *The plain sc rows are the right side of this piece. Push bobbles toward the back (which is the RS) as you work them.*

DOUBLE CROCHET 4 TOGETHER (bobble) (Yo, insert hook in next stitch, yo, draw yarn through stitch, yo, draw yarn through 2 lps on hook) 4 times in same stitch, yo, draw yarn through 5 lps on hook.

Ch a multiple of 4 stitches.

ROW 1 (RS) Ch 3 (counts as dc), dc in 4th ch from hook, dc in each ch across, turn.

ROW 2 (WS) Ch 1, sc in each of first 2 sc, *bobble in next sc, sc in each of next 3 sc; repeat from * across, ending with sc in each of last 2 sc, turn.

ROW 3 (RS) Ch 1, sc in each stitch across, turn.

ROW 4 (WS) Ch 1, sc in each of first 4 sc, *bobble in next sc, sc in each of next 3 sc; repeat from * across, ending with sc in each of last 4 sc, turn.

ROW 5 (RS) Ch 1, sc in each stitch across, turn.

Repeat Rows 2–5 for pattern, ending with Row 2 or 4.

LAST ROW Ch 3, sk first sc, dc in each stitch across. Fasten off.

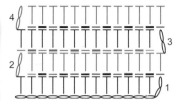

STITCH KEY

- ⬯ = chain (ch)
- T = half double crochet (hdc)
- — = worked in back loop only
- ▬ = worked in front loop only

Waffle Stitch (Half Double Crochet in Alternating Loops)

Ch a multiple of 2 stitches plus 1.
ROW 1 (RS) Ch 2 (counts as hdc throughout), hdc in 3rd ch from hook, hdc in each ch across, turn.

ROW 2 Ch 2, hdc in BL of next stitch, *hdc in FL of next stitch, hdc in BL of next st; repeat from * across, turn.

Repeat Row 2.

VARIATIONS: *Try this with sc, hdc, or tr stitches, using the appropriate number of turning chains for each stitch at the beginning of each row.*

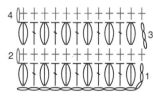

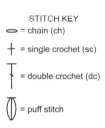

STITCH KEY
- ⬯ = chain (ch)
- + = single crochet (sc)
- T = double crochet (dc)
- ⬭ = puff stitch

Puff Stitch

PUFF STITCH (Yo, insert hook in next stitch, yo and draw up a lp) 3 times in same stitch, yo, and draw a lp through all 7 lps on hook, ch 1 tightly to secure.

Ch a multiple of 2 stitches plus 1.
ROW 1 (RS) Ch 3 (counts as dc throughout), puff stitch in 4th ch from hook, *dc in next ch, puff stitch in next ch; repeat from * across, turn.

ROW 2(WS) Ch 1, sc in each stitch across, turn.

ROW 3 (RS) Ch 3, sk first sc, puff stitch in next sc, *dc in next sc, puff stitch in next sc; repeat from * across, turn.

Repeat Rows 2 and 3.

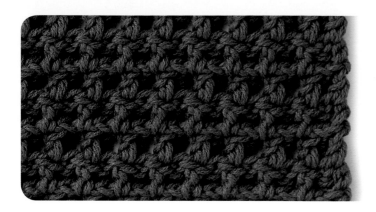

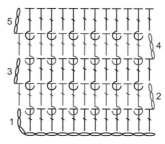

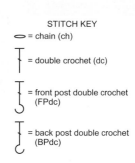

Double Crochet Rib

FRONT POST DOUBLE CROCHET (FPdc)
Yo, insert hook from front to back to front around the post of next dc, yo, draw up a lp, (yo, draw yarn through 2 lps on hook) twice.

BACK POST DOUBLE CROCHET (BPdc)
Yo, insert hook from back to front to back around the post of next dc, yo, draw up a lp, (yo, draw yarn through 2 lps on hook) twice.

NOTE: *Be careful not to make extra stitches in the top of the dc where you are making the FPdc or BPdc stitches. The side with the FPdc stitches is the right side of the work.*

Ch a multiple of 2 stitches.

ROW 1 (WS) Ch 3 (counts as dc throughout), dc in 4th ch from hook, dc in each ch across, turn.

ROW 2 (RS) Ch 3, sk first dc, *FPdc around the post of next stitch, dc in next stitch; repeat from * across, turn.

ROW 3 (WS) Ch 3, sk first dc, *BPdc around the post of next stitch, dc in next stitch; repeat from * across, turn.

Repeat Rows 2 and 3.

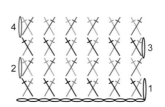

Crossed Single Crochet

Ch a multiple of 2 stitches.
ROW 1 (RS) Ch 1, sc in 3rd ch from hook, working around sc just made, sc in last ch skipped before sc just made, *sk next ch, sc in next ch, working around sc just made, sc in last skipped ch; repeat from * across, turn.

ROW 2 Ch 1, sk first sc, sc in next sc, working around sc just made, sc in last skipped sc, *sk next sc, sc in next sc, working around sc just made, sc in last skipped sc; repeat from * across, turn.

Repeat Row 2.

VARIATIONS: *Try this stitch pattern with dc and tr stitches, using the appropriate number of turning chains for each stitch at the beginning of each row.*

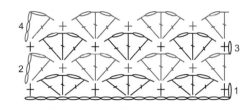

Floret Stitch

Ch a multiple of 6 stitches plus 1.

ROW 1 (RS) Ch 1, sc in 2nd ch from hook, *sk next 2 ch, (dc, ch 1, dc, ch 1, dc) in next ch, sk next 2 ch, sc in next ch; repeat from * across, turn.

ROW 2 (WS) Ch 4 (counts as dc, ch 1), dc in first sc, sk next dc, sc in next dc, *(dc, ch 1, dc, ch 1, dc) in next sc, sk next dc, sc in next dc; repeat from * across, ending with (dc, ch 1, dc) in last sc, turn.

ROW 3 (RS) Ch 1, sc in first dc, *(dc, ch 1, dc, ch 1, dc) in next sc, sk next dc, sc in next dc; repeat from * across, ending with sc in 3rd ch of turning ch, turn.

Repeat Rows 2 and 3.

STITCH KEY
⬯ = chain (ch)
+ = single crochet (sc)
⊤ = double crochet (dc)

Mesh and Netting

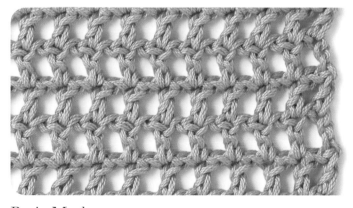

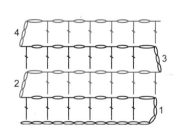

Basic Mesh

Ch a multiple of 2 stitches.

ROW 1 (RS) Ch 4 (counts as dc, ch 1 throughout), dc in 6th ch from hook, *ch 1, sk next ch, dc in next ch; repeat from * across, turn.

ROW 2 (WS) Ch 4, sk next ch-1 sp, dc in next dc, *ch 1, sk next ch-1 sp, dc in next dc; repeat from * across, ending with dc in 3rd ch of turning ch, turn.

Repeat Row 2.

STITCH KEY
⬯ = chain (ch)
⊤ = double crochet (dc)

VARIATIONS: *Replace the dc with sc, hdc, or tr stitches, making sure to include the appropriate number of turning chains at the beginning of each row.*

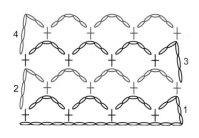

Fishnet

Ch a multiple of 4 stitches plus 3.

ROW 1 (RS) Ch 5, sc in 8th ch from hook, *ch 5, sk next 3 ch, sc in next ch; repeat from * across, turn.

ROW 2 (WS) Ch 5, (sc, ch 5) in each ch–5 lp across, ending with sc in 3rd ch of turning ch, turn.

Repeat row 2.

VARIATIONS: *Try increasing the number of chains between single crochets, or replace ch-5 lps with (ch 2, dc in sc, ch 2).*

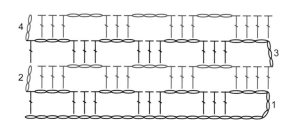

Checkerboard

Ch a multiple of 6 stitches plus 4.

ROW 1 (RS) Ch 6, dc in 10th ch from hook, dc in each of next 2 ch, *ch 3, sk next 3 ch, dc in each of next 3 ch; repeat from * across to within last 4 ch, ch 3, sk next 3 ch, dc in last ch, turn.

ROW 2 (WS) Ch 3 (counts as dc here and throughout), dc in each of next 3 ch, *ch 3, sk next 3 dc, dc in each of next 3 ch; repeat from * across, ending with dc in top of turning ch, turn.

ROW 3 (RS) Ch 6 (counts as dc, ch 3 here and throughout), sk next 3 dc, *dc in each of next 3 ch, ch 3, sk next 3 dc; repeat from * across, ending with dc in top of turning ch.

Repeat Rows 2 and 3.

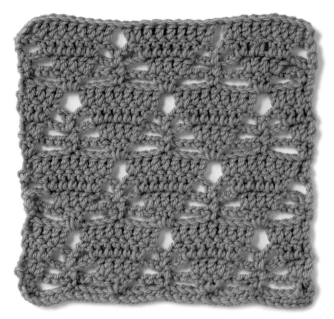

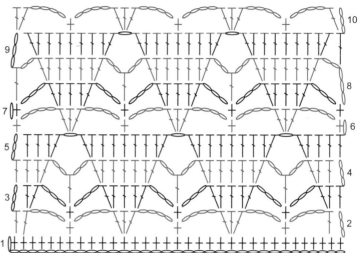

Embedded Triangles

Ch a multiple of 10 stitches plus 3.

ROW 1 (WS) Ch 1, sc in 2nd ch from hook, sc in each ch across, turn.

ROW 2 (RS) Ch 3 (counts as dc throughout), sk first sc, dc in next sc, *ch 4, sk next 4 sc, sc in next sc, ch 4, sk next 4 sc**, 3 dc in next sc; repeat from * across, ending last repeat at **, dc in each of last 2 sc, turn.

ROW 3 (WS) Ch 3, sk first dc, *2 dc in next dc, ch 3, sk next ch-4 sp, sc in next sc, ch 3, sk next ch-4 sp, 2 dc in next dc, dc in next dc; repeat from * across, ending with last dc in top of turning ch, turn.

ROW 4 (RS) Ch 3, sk first dc, dc in next dc, *2 dc in next dc, ch 2, sk next ch-3 sp, dc in next sc, ch 2, sk next ch-3 sp, 2 dc in next dc**, dc in each of next 3 dc; repeat from * across, ending last repeat at **, dc in next dc, dc in top of turning ch, turn.

ROW 5 (WS) Ch 3, sk first dc, dc in each of next 2 dc, 2 dc in next dc, *ch 1, sk next 2 ch-2 sps, 2 dc in next dc**, dc in each of next 5 dc, 2 dc in next dc; repeat from * across, ending last repeat at **, dc in last 2 dc and in top of turning ch, turn.

ROW 6 (RS) Ch 1, sc in first dc, *ch 4, sk next 4 dc, 3 dc in next ch-1 sp, ch 4, sk next 4 dc, sc in next dc; repeat from * across, ending with last sc in top of turning ch, turn.

ROW 7 (WS) Ch 1, sc in first sc, *ch 3, sk next ch-4 sp, 2 dc in next dc, dc in next dc, 2 dc in next dc, ch 3, sk next ch-4 sp, sc in next sc; repeat from * across, turn.

ROW 8 (RS) Ch 5 (counts as dc, ch 2), *sk next ch-3 sp, 2 dc in next dc, dc in each of next 3 dc, 2 dc in next dc, ch 2, sk next ch-3 sp, dc in next sc**, ch 2; repeat from * across, ending last repeat at **, turn.

ROW 9 (WS) Ch 3, sk next ch-2 sp, *2 dc in next dc, dc in each of next 5 dc, 2 dc in next dc**, ch 1, sk next 2 ch-2 sps; repeat from * across, ending last repeat at **, sk next ch-2 sp, dc in 3rd ch of turning ch, turn.

ROW 10 (RS) Ch 3, dc in first dc, *ch 4, sk next 4 dc, sc in next dc, ch 4, sk next 4 dc**, 3 dc in next ch-1 sp; repeat from * across, ending last repeat at **, 2 dc in top of turning ch, turn.

Repeat Rows 3–10.

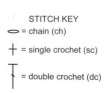

STITCH KEY

⬯ = chain (ch)

+ = single crochet (sc)

⊺ = double crochet (dc)

STITCH KEY

⬭ = chain (ch)

+ = single crochet (sc)

⊤ = double crochet (dc)

⊤ = double treble crochet
(dtr)

Embedded Squares

DOUBLE TREBLE CROCHET (dtr) Yo 3 times, insert hook in next stitch, yo and draw up a lp, (yo, draw through 2 lps on hook) 4 times.

Ch a multiple of 14 stitches plus 1.

ROW 1 (RS) Ch 1, sc in 2nd ch from hook, *ch 4, sk next 4 ch, dtr in each of next 5 ch, ch 4, sk next 4 ch, sc in next ch; repeat from * across, turn.

ROW 2 (WS) Ch 6 (counts as dc, ch 3 here and throughout), (sc, ch 5) in each ch-4 lp across, ending with sc in last ch-4 lp, ch 3, dc in last sc, turn.

ROW 3 (RS) Ch 5, 2 dtr in next ch-3 sp, *ch 4, sc in next ch-5 lp, ch 4, 5 dtr in next ch-5 lp; repeat from * across, ending with 3 dtr in turning ch-lp, turn.

ROW 4 (WS) Ch 6, (sc, ch 5) in each ch-4 lp across, ending with ch 3, sk next 2 dtr, dc in top of turning ch, turn.

ROW 5 (RS) Ch 1, sc in first dc, sk next ch-3 sp, *ch 4, 5 dtr in next ch-5 lp, ch 4, sc in next ch-5 sp; repeat from * across, ending with last sc in 3rd ch of turning ch, turn.

Repeat Rows 2–5.

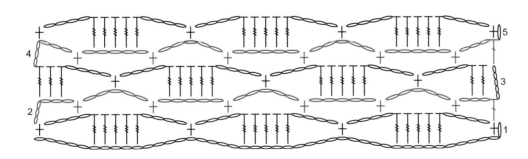

Shells, Scallops, and Lace

Asymmetrical Shells

Ch a multiple of 7 stitches plus 1.

ROW 1 (RS) Ch 3 (counts as dc throughout), (4 dc, ch 2, dc) in 7th ch from hook, *sk next 6 ch, (4 dc, ch 2, dc) in next ch; repeat from * across to within last 4 ch, sk next 3 ch, dc in last ch, turn.

ROW 2 (WS) Ch 3, sk first 2 dc, *(4 dc, ch 2, dc) in next ch-2 sp, sk next 5 dc; repeat from * across, ending with dc in top of turning ch.

Repeat Row 2.

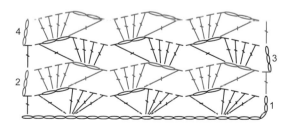

Strawberry Stitch

TREBLE 3 TOGETHER CLUSTER (tr3tog) (Yo twice, insert hook in stitch, yo, draw yarn through stitch, [yo, draw yarn through 2 lps on hook] twice) 3 times in same stitch, yo, draw yarn through 4 lps on hook.

Ch a multiple of 16 stitches plus 6.

ROW 1 (RS) Ch 3 (counts as dc throughout), (3 dc, ch 2, 3 dc) in 5th ch from hook, *ch 4, sk next 7 ch, (dc, ch 4, dc) in next ch, ch 4, sk next 7 ch, (3 dc, ch 2, 3 dc) in next ch; repeat from * across to within last 3 ch, sk next 2 ch, dc in last ch, turn.

ROW 2 (WS) Ch 3, sk first 4 dc, *(3 dc, ch 2, 3 dc) in next ch-2 sp, ch 2, sk ch-4 sp, ([tr3tog, ch 3] 3 times, tr3tog) in next ch-4 sp, ch 2, sk next ch-4 sp; repeat from * across, ending with (3 dc, ch 2, 3 dc) in last ch-2 sp, dc in top of turning ch, turn.

ROW 3 (RS) Ch 3, sk first 4 dc, *(3 dc, ch 2, 3 dc) in next ch-2 sp, ch 3, sk next ch-2 sp, (2 sc, ch 3) in each of next 3 ch-3 sps, sk next ch-2 sp; repeat from * across, ending with (3 dc, ch 2, 3 dc) in last ch-2 sp, dc in top of turning ch, turn.

ROW 4 (WS) Ch 3, sk first 4 dc, *(3 dc, ch 2, 3 dc) in next ch-2 sp, ch 4, sk next ch-3 sp, 2 sc in next ch-3 sp, ch 3, 2 sc in next ch-3 sp, ch 4, sk next ch-3 sp; repeat from * across, ending with (3 dc, ch 2, 3 dc) in last ch-2 sp, dc in top of turning ch, turn.

ROW 5 (RS) Ch 3, sk first 4 dc, *(3 dc, ch 2, 3 dc) in next ch-2 sp, ch 4, sk next ch-4 sp, (dc, ch 4, dc) in next ch-3 sp, ch 4, sk next ch-4 sp; repeat from * across, ending with (3 dc, ch 2, 3 dc) in last ch-2 sp, dc in top of turning ch, turn.

Repeat Rows 2–5, ending with Row 4.

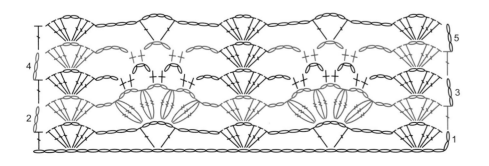

STITCH KEY
◠ = chain (ch)
+ = single crochet (sc)
T = double crochet (dc)
= tr3tog

Daisy Lace

PICOT Ch 4, sl st into first ch.

Ch a multiple of 4 stitches.

ROW 1 (RS) Ch 1, make 3 picots, sk 2 ch, *sc in each of next 3 ch, make 3 picots, sk next ch; repeat from * across, ending with sc in each of last 3 ch, picot, turn.

ROW 2 (WS) Ch 3, picot, *ch 3, picot, make 2 ch of next picot, sc in center picot of corresponding 3-picot group in row below, ch 2 for 2nd half of picot, rotate last picot down, bring yarn to front of work, sl st in 4th ch from hook to finish picot, work one more picot; repeat from * across, work 2 more picots, turn.

ROW 3 (RS) Rotating picots down as you crochet, *sc in each of next 3 ch of ch-3 sp between picots**, work 3 picots; repeat from * across, ending last repeat at **, picot, turn.

Repeat Rows 2 and 3.

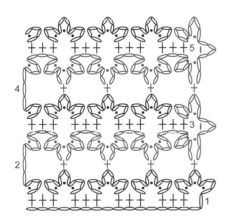

STITCH KEY
- ⬯ = chain (ch)
- • = slip st (sl st)
- ✛ = single crochet (sc)
- 🞡 = picot

Cluster Flowers

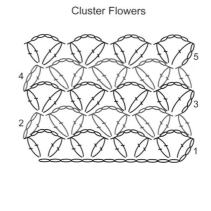

STITCH KEY

⬯ = chain (ch)

T = double crochet (dc)

⬥ = dc2tog

Cluster Flowers

DOUBLE CROCHET 2 TOGETHER CLUSTER (dc2tog) (Yo, insert hook in next stitch, yo, draw yarn through stitch, yo, draw yarn through 2 lps on hook) twice in same stitch, yo, draw yarn through 3 lps on hook.

Ch a multiple of 4 stitches plus 1.

ROW 1 (RS) Ch 3, (dc, ch 4, dc2tog) in 4th ch from hook (counts as dc2tog, ch 4, dc2tog here and throughout), *sk next 3 ch, (dc2tog, ch 4, dc2tog) in next ch; repeat from * across, turn.

ROW 2 (WS) Ch 3, dc in first stitch (counts as dc2tog), *sk next ch-4 lp and next dc2tog, (dc2tog, ch 4, dc2tog) in top of next dc2tog; repeat from * across, ending with dc2tog in last dc.

ROW 3 (RS) Ch 3, sk first dc2tog, (dc, ch 4, dc2tog) in top of next dc2tog, *sk next ch-4 lp and next dc2tog, (dc2tog, ch 4, dc2tog) in next dc2tog; repeat from * across, ending with (dc2tog, ch 4, dc2tog) in last dc, turn.

Repeat Rows 2 and 3.

Pretty Pineapples

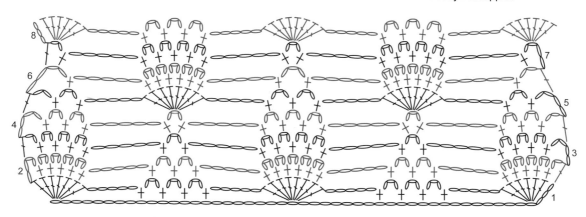

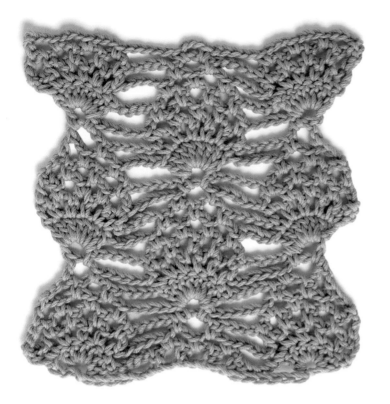

STITCH KEY

⬯ = chain (ch)

✛ = single crochet (sc)

⊤ = double crochet (dc)

Pretty Pineapples

Ch a multiple of 22 stitches plus 1.

ROW 1 (RS) Ch 3 (counts as first dc), 6 dc in 4th ch from hook, *ch 5, sk next 7 ch, sc in next ch, (ch 3, sk next ch, sc in next ch) 3 times, ch 5, sk next 7 ch, 8 dc in next ch; repeat from * across, ending with 7 dc in last ch, turn.

ROW 2 (WS) Ch 4, sk first dc, sc in next dc, (ch 3, sc) in each of next 4 dc, *ch 5, sk ch-5 lp, (sc, ch 3) in each of next 2 ch-3 sps, sc in next ch-3 sp, ch 5, sk next ch-5 lp, sk next dc, sc in next dc, (ch 3, sc) in each of next 5 dc; repeat from * across, omitting last (ch-3, sc), ending with ch 2, dc in top of turning ch, turn.

ROW 3 (RS) Ch 4, sk next ch-2 sp, (sc, ch 3) in each of next 3 ch-3 sps, sc in next ch-3 sp, *ch 5, sk next ch-5 lp, sc in next ch-3 sp, ch 3, sc in next ch-3 sp, ch 5, sk next ch-5 lp, (sc, ch 3) in each of next 4 ch-3 sps, sc in next ch-3 sp; repeat from * across, omitting last (ch-3 sc), ending with ch 3, dc in top of turning ch, turn.

ROW 4 (WS) Ch 4, sk next ch-2 sp, (sc, ch 3) in each of next 2 ch-3 sps, sc in next ch-3 sp, *ch 5, sk next ch-5 lp, (sc, ch 3, sc) in next ch-3 sp, ch 5, sk next ch-5 lp, (sc, ch 3) in each of next 3 ch-3 sps, sc in next ch-3 sp; repeat from * across, omitting last (ch-3 sc), ending with ch 2, dc in top of turning ch, turn.

ROW 5 (RS) Ch 4, sk next ch-2 sp, sc in next ch-3 sp, ch 3, sc in next ch-3 sp, *ch 5, sk next ch-5 lp, 8 dc in next ch-3 sp, ch 5, sk next ch-5 lp, (sc, ch 3) in each of next 2 ch-3 sps, sc in next ch-3 sp; repeat from * across, omitting last (ch-3 sc), ending with ch 2, dc in top of turning ch, turn.

ROW 6 (WS) Ch 4, sk next ch-2 sp, sc in next ch-3 sp, *ch 5, sk next ch-5 lp, sk next dc, (sc, ch 3) in each of next 5 dc, sc in next dc, ch 5, sk next ch-5 lp, sc in next ch-3 sp, ch 3, sc in next ch-3 sp; repeat from * across, omitting last (ch-3 sc), ending with ch 2, dc in top of turning ch, turn.

ROW 7 (RS) Ch 4, sc in next ch-2 sp, *ch 5, sk next ch-5 lp, (sc, ch 3) in each of next 4 ch-3 sps, sc in next ch-3 sp, ch 5, sk next ch-5 lp**, (sc, ch 3, sc) in next ch-3 sp; repeat from * across, ending last repeat at **, (sc, ch 2, dc) in turning ch lp, turn.

ROW 8 (WS) Ch 3, 6 dc in next ch-2 sp, *ch 5, sk next ch-5 lp, (sc, ch 3) in each of next 3 ch-3 sps, sc in next ch-3 sp, ch 5, sk next ch-5 lp, 8 dc in next ch-3 sp; repeat from * across, ending with 7 dc in turning ch lp, turn.

Repeat Rows 2–8, ending with Row 4 or 6.

Colorwork

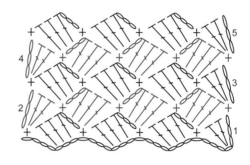

Tumbling Blocks

Ch a multiple of 7 stitches plus 5.

ROW 1 (RS) Ch 3 (counts as dc), 2 dc in 4th ch from hook, *sk next 3 ch, sc in next ch, ch 3, dc in each of next 3 ch; repeat from * across to within last 4 ch, ending with sk next 3 ch, sc in last ch, turn.

ROW 2 (WS) Ch 3, 2 dc in first sc, *sk next 3 dc, sc in next ch, ch 3, dc in each of next 2 ch, dc in next sc; repeat from * across to within last 3 stitches, ending with sk 2 dc, sc in top of turning ch, turn.

Repeat Row 2.

STITCH KEY

⬯ = chain (ch)

+ = single crochet (sc)

† = double crochet (dc)

Ripple

DOUBLE CROCHET 2 TOGETHER SPACE (dc2tog) (Yo, insert hook in next stitch, yo, draw yarn through stitch, yo, draw yarn through 2 lps on hook), sk next stitch, (yo, insert hook in next stitch, yo, draw yarn through stitch, yo, draw yarn through 2 lps on hook), yo, draw yarn through 3 lps on hook.

Ch a multiple of 12 stitches plus 1.

ROW 1 (RS) Ch 3 (counts as dc throughout), dc in 4th ch from hook, *dc in each of next 4 ch, (dc2tog, worked across next 3 ch), dc in each of next 4 ch**, (dc, ch 1, dc) in next ch; repeat from * across, ending last repeat at **, 2 dc in last ch, turn.

ROW 2 (WS) Ch 3, dc in first dc, *dc in each of next 4 dc, (dc2tog, worked across next 3 stitches), dc in each of next 4 dc**, (dc, ch 1, dc) in next ch-1 sp; repeat from * across, ending last repeat at **, 2 dc in top of turning ch.

Repeat Row 2.

VARIATIONS: *For a closed ripple, replace each dc2tog with dc3tog in each valley; replace each (dc, ch 1, dc) with 3 dc in ch-1 sps at each peak.*

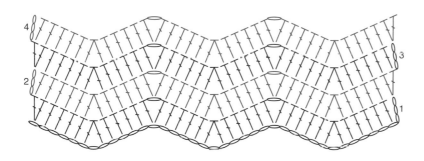

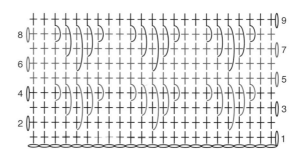

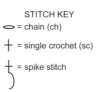

STITCH KEY
⬭ = chain (ch)

╋ = single crochet (sc)

╋ = spike stitch

Wavy Spikes

NOTE: *A spike stitch is worked one or more rows beneath the working row to add a splash of color—keep your tension loose when working spike stitches to account for the height of the stitch.*

SPIKE SINGLE CROCHET 1 (ssc1) Insert hook in next corresponding sc one row below, yo, draw yarn through stitch and up to level of work, yo, draw yarn through 2 lps on hook.

SPIKE SINGLE CROCHET 2 (ssc2) Insert hook in next corresponding sc 2 rows below, yo, draw yarn through stitch and up to level of work, yo, draw yarn through 2 lps on hook.

SPIKE SINGLE CROCHET 3 (SSC3) Insert hook in next corresponding sc 3 rows below, yo, draw yarn through stitch and up to level of work, yo, draw yarn through 2 lps on hook.

With first color, ch a multiple of 7 stitches plus 2.
ROW 1 (RS) Ch 1, sc in 2nd ch from hook, sc in each ch across, turn.
ROWS 2–4 Ch 1, sc in each sc across, turn. At end of row 4, fasten off first color, join 2nd color.

ROW 5 (RS) Ch 1, sc in first 2 sc, *SSC1 over next st, SSC2 over next stitch, SSC3 over next st, SSC2 over next stitch, SSC1 over next stitch, sc in each of next 2 sc; repeat from * across, turn.
ROWS 6–8 Repeat row 2. At end of row 8, fasten off 2nd color, join first color.
ROW 9 (RS) Repeat Row 5.

Repeat Rows 2–9, changing colors as indicated.

VARIATIONS: *Try clustering the spike stitches or varying their lengths to form different patterns.*

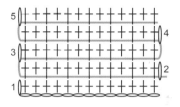

STITCH KEY

⬭ = chain (ch)

+ = single crochet (sc)

— = carried 2nd color

Running Stitch

NOTE: *This running stitch is made as you crochet by alternately crocheting over the contrasting yarn and letting the yarn sit in front (on RS rows) or in back (on WS rows) of the stitch.*

With first color, ch a multiple of 2 stitches plus 1.

ROW 1 (WS) Ch 1, sc in 2nd ch from hook, sc in each stitch across, turn.

ROW 2 (RS) Hold 2nd color over the first row of stitches, leaving a long tail hanging at the right-side edge of the work. With first color, ch 1, sc over 2nd color, *bring 2nd color strand to the front of the work, being careful not to catch 2nd color, sc in next sc; sc over 2nd color in next sc, pull 2nd color taut; repeat from * across, turn, leaving 2nd color strand at back of work.

ROW 3 (WS) With first color, ch 1, sc over 2nd color, *bring 2nd color strand to the back of the work, being careful not to catch 2nd color, sc in next sc; sc over 2nd color in next sc, pull 2nd color taut; repeat from * across, turn, leaving 2nd color strand at front of work.

Repeat Rows 2 and 3. Fasten off 2nd color, leaving a long tail.

LAST ROW (RS) With first color, ch 1, sc in each sc across. Fasten off first color.

VARIATIONS: *Replace Row 3 with a row of sc over 2nd color for a running stitch on alternate rows only.*

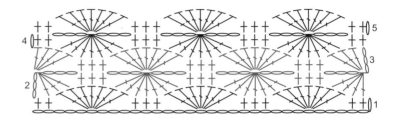

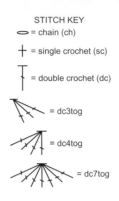

STITCH KEY

◯ = chain (ch)

+ = single crochet (sc)

┃ = double crochet (dc)

⋏ = dc3tog

⋏ = dc4tog

⋏ = dc7tog

Catherine Wheel

DOUBLE CROCHET 3 TOGETHER (dc3tog)
(Yo, insert hook in next stitch, yo, draw yarn through stitch, yo, draw yarn through 2 lps on hook) 3 times, yo, draw yarn through 4 lps on hook.

DOUBLE CROCHET 4 TOGETHER (dc4tog)
(Yo, insert hook in next stitch, yo, draw yarn through stitch, yo, draw yarn through 2 lps on hook) 4 times, yo, draw yarn through 5 lps on hook.

DOUBLE CROCHET 7 TOGETHER (dc7tog)
(Yo, insert hook in next stitch, yo, draw yarn through stitch, yo, draw yarn through 2 lps on hook) 7 times, yo, draw yarn through 8 lps on hook.

With first color, ch a multiple of 10 stitches plus 1.

ROW 1 (RS) Ch 1, sc in 2nd ch from hook, sc in next ch, *sk next 3 ch, 7 dc in next ch, sk next 3 ch**, sc in each of next 3 ch; repeat from * across, ending last repeat at **, sc in each of last 2 ch, turn. Fasten off first color, join 2nd color.

ROW 2 (WS) With 2nd color, ch 3 (counts as dc throughout), sk first sc, dc3tog over next 3 stitches, *ch 3, sc in each of next 3 dc, ch 3**, dc7tog over next 7 stitches; repeat from * across, ending last repeat at **, dc4tog over last 4 stitches, turn.

ROW 3 (RS) Ch 3, 3 dc in first dc4tog, *sk next ch-3 sp, sc in each of next 3 sc, sk next ch-3 sp**, 7 dc in next dc7tog; repeat from * across, ending last repeat at **, 4 dc in last dc4tog, turn. Fasten off 2nd color, join first color.

ROW 4 (WS) With first color, ch 1, sc in first 2 sc, *ch 3, dc7tog over next 7 stitches, ch 3**, sc in each of next 3 dc; repeat from * across, ending last repeat at **, sc in each of last 2 stitches, turn.

ROW 5 (RS) Ch 1, sc in each of first 2 sc, *sk next ch-3 sp, 7 dc in next dc7tog, sk next ch-3 sp**, sc in each of next 3 sc; repeat from * across, ending last repeat at **, sc in each of last 2 sc, turn. Fasten off first color, join 2nd color.

Repeat Rows 2–5.

VARIATIONS: *To incorporate more colors, use a 3rd color for rows 4 and 5 and change colors every two rows.*

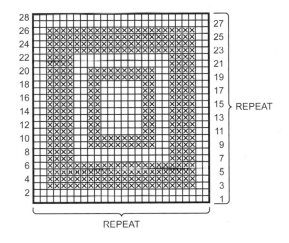

Cross Stitch on Single Crochet

Ch 28 stitches for each pattern.

Background

ROW 1 (RS) Ch 1, sc in 2nd ch from hook, sc in each ch across, turn.

ROWS 2–28 Ch 1, sc in each sc across, turn.

Work 28 rows of Row 2 for each pattern repeat. Fasten off.

Embroidery

With 2nd color and yarn needle, cross stitch over the sc background following the chart.

CHART KEY
☐ = background sc
☒ = cross stitch

Resources

All of the materials in this book should be available at your local craft stores and yarn shops. The following list of suppliers will help you locate the supplies you need to complete the projects in the book—consult their websites to find a distributor near you.

YARN

Thanks to the following companies for the use of their gorgeous fibers and crochet accessories.

Berroco
PO Box 367
14 Elmdale Road
Uxbridge, MA 01569
508-278-2527
www.berroco.com

Blue Sky Alpacas, Inc.
PO Box 88
Cedar, MN 55011
888-460-8862
www.blueskyalpacas.com

Brown Sheep Company, Inc.
100662 County Road 16
Mitchell, NE 69357
800-826-9136
www.brownsheep.com

Cascade Yarns
PO Box 58168
Tukwila, WA 98138
800-548-1048
www.cascadeyarns.com

Coats & Clark
Attn: Consumer Services
P.O. Box 12229
Greenville, SC 29612
800-648-1479
www.coatsandclark.com

Fiesta Yarns
5401 San Diego NE
Albuquerque, NM 87113
505-892-5008
www.fiestayarns.com

Lion Brand Yarn Co.
135 Kero Road
Carlstadt, NJ 07072
800-795-5466
www.lionbrand.com

Louet North America
808 Commerce Park Drive
Ogdensburg, NY 13669
613-925-4502
www.louet.com

Muench Yarns, Inc.
1323 Scott Street
Petaluma, CA 94954
800-733-9276
www.muenchyarns.com

Southwest Trading Company
918 S. Park Lane, Suite 102
Tempe, AZ 85281
866-794-1818
www.soysilk.com

Tahki Stacy Charles, Inc.
70-30 80th Street
Building 36
Ridgewood, NY 11385
800-338-YARN
www.tahkistacycharles.com

HOOKS AND NOTIONS

Clover
www.clover-usa.com

Michaels
8000 Bent Branch Dr.
Irving, TX 75063
800-Michaels
www.michaels.com

Susan Bates
www.coatsandclark.com

Unique Stitch Fabric Glue
www.mjtrim.com

Wrights (Boye Crochet Hooks)
www.wrights.com

FABRIC

If you're looking for a great fabric to go with your project, check out these online retailers.

eBay
Search this auction site if you're looking for a specific fabric that has been discontinued, large lots of vintage fabric scraps or doilies, or any craft supply your heart desires.
www.ebay.com

Etsy

Home to unique handspun yarns, fabric yardage and handmade goodies.
www.etsy.com

Jo-Ann Fabric and Craft Stores

5555 Darrow Rd.
Hudson, OH 44236
888-739-4120
www.joann.com

Purl Soho

Yarn, fabric, and all the tools you'll need, all in one spot.
www.purlsoho.com

ReproDepot

A great mix of retro-inspired fabrics.
www.reprodepot.com

Sew Mama Sew

A wonderful collection of modern and vintage-inspired prints, and you can buy in quantities of less than a yard.
www.sewmamasew.com

HELPFUL WEBSITES

Crochet Guild of America

A nonprofit association dedicated to preserving and advancing the art of crochet. Visit their website to find a local chapter of crocheters.
www.crochet.org

Craft Yarn Council

A helpful resource for information on understanding patterns, standard size measurements, and more.
www.yarnstandards.com

Online Crochet and Craft Communities

Craftster

Surf this heavily used site for all things crafty; you're sure to find a home on the crochet forum.
www.craftster.org

Craft Stylish

Browse this site for weekly updates full of crochet tips, tricks, and techniques.
www.craftstylish.com

Crochet Me

User-driven tips, techniques, and patterns.
www.crochetme.com

Crochetville

Here you can join a crochet-along, take online classes, or discuss your latest crochet project.
www.crochetville.org

Ravelry

This amazing site lists a host of crochet and knitting patterns from magazines, books, websites, and more. Post your finished projects here and see how other people interpret the same instructions.
www.ravelry.com

FURTHER READING

These titles will help you expand your stitch repertoire or refresh your skills.

Books

Chan, Doris. 2007. *Everyday Crochet.* New York: Potter Craft.

Kagan, Sasha. 2007. *Crochet Inspiration* New York: Sixth and Spring.

Kooler, Donna. 2002. *Encyclopedia of Crochet.* Little Rock: Leisure Arts.

Stoller, Debbie. 2006. *Stitch 'N Bitch Crochet: The Happy Hooker.* New York: Workman.

The Harmony Guides. 1999. *300 Crochet Stitches* (The Harmony Guides, vol. 6). London: Collins and Brown.

The Harmony Guides. 1999. *220 More Crochet Stitches* (The Harmony Guides, vol. 6). London: Collins and Brown.

Magazines

Crochet Today! magazine.
www.crochettoday.com

Interweave Crochet magazine.
www.interweavecrochet.com

Acknowledgments

First off, I'd like to thank all of the yarn companies who sent me their wonderful fibers, especially Cascade Yarns, Coats and Clark, and Louet, all of whom provided the yarns featured in the stitch dictionary. Thanks also to Tanis Gray at *Vogue Knitting* for helping me with her industry knowledge.

My sincere gratitude goes to the talented crocheters who contributed their designs and their time to this book. Thanks to Tricia Royal for designing the Mod Cross Pillow (page 88), Diane Gilleland for her Vintage Kitchen Trivets (page 91), and Megan Granholm, who stitched the swatches for the stitch pattern section of the dictionary. To my wonderful tech editor and diagram maker, Karen Manthey—I could not have done it without you!

I'd also like to thank Susan Beal for nudging me to write this book, and introducing me to my agent, Stacey Glick—thanks Stacey, for sealing the deal! To Christina Batch, Brett Bara, and Trisha Malcolm—thanks for all the fun we had making magazines. And to the wonderful people at Potter Craft who helped me to make this book: Jennifer Graham for her keen attention to detail, Melissa Bonventre for her marketing expertise, and Kara Plikaitis and Chi Ling Moy for their design sense. Thanks also to Heather Weston for the adorable photography and Lana Le for the helpful illustrations throughout the book.

To all of my crafty supporters on the Internet—thank you, thank you, thank you for all of your comments and cheerleading, not to mention all of the inspiring posts you write.

And of course, thanks go to my partner, Paul Heaston, who put up with our couch being covered with yarn and books for months (I'll move them, I swear!) and often still finds yarn tails in the strangest places. I love you.

Last but not least, sincere thanks go to my family, especially my mom, for always listening.

Index